2005
124

abc
of 20th-century graphics

Coordinating Editor
Giovanna Crespi
Translation
Christopher Evans
Richard Sadleir
Graphic Design and Layout
Tassinari/Vetta
Cover Graphics
Tassinari/Vetta
Page Layout
Eva Bozzi
Editing
Gail Swerling
Technical Coordination
Paolo Verri
Andrea Panozzo

Distributed by Phaidon Press
ISBN 1-904313-24-8

www.phaidon.com

www.electaweb.it

Printed in China

abc

of 20th-century graphics
text by sergio polano
illustrations compiled by pierpaolo vetta

Electaarchitecture

Contents

Preface

This volume contains a coherent selection of the many essays, generally of a historical character and often aimed at a general readership, that I have written over the last decade, at different times and in different circumstances, on the themes of *graphics* and *images*, *scripts* and *lettering*. Some were delivered as lectures and a few have never previously been published, while others have already appeared several times, as will be apparent from the publishing credits at the back of the book. I take a very broad approach to these subjects, as can be seen from the three definitions or glosses that follow this preface and are meant to give readers some critical guidance.

Pierpaolo Vetta undertook to provide the volume with a suitable set of illustrations and captions that would illuminate its contents and point up the arguments presented in the various essays.

Far from making any pretense to offering a systematic history of contemporary graphics, the very nature of the texts, reprinted as they first appeared with a few slight changes where necessary, means that the anthology falls into two parts. The first is organized around themes and concepts, with the essays arranged to reflect the content; the second centers on leading figures and its arrangement is broadly chronological.

The first part, "Typology" explores the features of the "word made visible" (ranging from calligraphy to digital type) in the dialectic between the method used to trace the marks and the surface on which they are traced; at the same time it looks ahead to the advent of that *neography* that—with secret satisfaction—I have discovered was also proposed by Roland Barthes.

"Paper Architecture" looks at the history of one of the commonest and most interesting of graphic artifacts, the postage stamp.

"Talking Figures" investigates the meaning and role of illustrations. "The Return of Pictograms" is dedicated to a distinctive form of icon (signs, pictograms). "Notes towards an imaginary chapter in a history of visual thinking…" is a deliberately fragmentary treatment of posters, bills, placards or whatever one chooses to call them. The great digital melting pot of this new form of communication and its possible outcomes are the themes of "Digital Soup."

In the light of the theories and themes discussed in Part I,
the historical approach in the second part proceeds by examples.
They begin in the first half of the 20th century with Peter Behrens
and are followed by the ground-breaking experiments of the great
Soviet Constructivists El Lissitzky and Alexander Rodchenko,
the Briton Eric Gill and the Germans Jan Tschichold and Kurt
Schwitters, as well as the Bauhaus, and culminate in Paul Renner
& Paul Rand. The chapter titled "Wolfgang Weingart" examines
the formation and consolidation of a specific tradition of
"systematic design," from the Nieuwe Beelding to the New Wave,
while the essay on Max Huber relates the little-known story
of his beginnings. Turning to the second half of the 20th century,
the examination of the masters resumes with Adrian Frutiger
and Aldo Novarese, with a discussion of some outstanding
typefaces, and proceeds with two more Italian masters,
Giovanni Pintori and Franco Grignani. The long text on Wim Crouwel
provides an opportunity to return to the subject of monoalphabets
and the Netherlands (while also suggesting a method
of investigating type design). The biographical study,
"Matthew Carter. A Man of Characters," is followed by essays on
Erik Spiekermann, tackling the themes of the identity of institutions
and urban communities, and the ineffable activities
of Tibor Kalman. The anthology concludes with the chapter
on Ed Fella, which discusses the vernacular in contemporary
American graphics.
Although in no way systematic, this collection of texts has a
general critical object, which runs through it like a fine guiding
thread: the attempt to set the activity commonly defined today
as "graphics" in what I believe (and I am certainly not alone)
is its true and proper context, in both historical and cultural terms.
In the history of "humanization," i.e. the long process of becoming
Homo (both *sapiens* and *faber*) by the particular species
of primates to which we belong, the tracing of graphic signs—at first
abstract, rhythmical-geometrical, then later figurative,
in the renowned cave paintings and many other prehistoric
artifacts—is a very distinctive aptitude (some scholars even believe
it preceded speech) that dates back to tens of thousands
of years BC. The spread of humanity over the earth is marked
by the "writing" of signs. They range from prehistoric signs
("prehistoric" only because of the absence of a codified script),

whose functions we are unable to understand (except conjecturally and then usually on conflicting and unresolved or even unhistorical grounds), to the great variety of forms in the contemporary world. Clearly the humanization of the world has consisted in making it more artificial, through the progressive construction and increasing specialization of families of artifacts, constructs that are to variable degrees both prosthetic/utilitarian and communicative/symbolic: garments, ornaments, buildings, carvings, paintings, tools, furniture, books, machines (the list could go on endlessly).
In this field, a historical investigation (of the visual arts in the strict sense), if it is to avoid narrowness, has to cope with a range of graphic artifacts that are immensely diverse and varied: in their medium of expression, the intentions of their creators, their social significance, technical forms, means of production and modes of reception. In this very broad development, the image (it is no coincidence that the word derives from a root that means "double") clearly becomes distinguished from writing and painting, activities that in Greek were still encompassed by the single word *graphein*.
Given these indispensable premises, the construction of a history of "graphics," which is what interests us here, can and should go its own way and identify the most significant developments.
One of these is the bumpy road that led from chiro-graphy (writing by hand) to typo-graphy and then to the complexities of the digital breakthrough in writing systems, essentially meaning alphabets for us Westerners. Then there is the related development of the formats, proportions and ways of organizing the support/surface (papyrus, parchment, paper or monitor, to cut the list very short) in relation to the figures/signs (images and letters) with which they are covered using highly specialized implements, methods and techniques of impression. Finally, among the many other points that really ought to be more widely understood, there is the pertinence of contemporary graphics to industrial design, and more precisely to visual design: a specific discipline, which requires appropriate training, aptitudes and instruments together with application, knowledge and study, all of which cannot be improvised and are not very common, though the confused ideas on the subject so common nowadays might suggest the opposite.

Sergio Polano

Image

The word comes from the Latin *imago*, linked with *imitari*, to imitate, whose root (attested in the Indo-Iranian, Baltic and Celtic areas) is *yem*: this has the meaning of double product, double fruit, twofold.

"The image, as sign, as an element in a system of communication," Roland Barthes has written in this connection, "makes a deep impression. Attempts have been made to study this shock value but we need to be very cautious: as sign, an image has one drawback, one considerable inconvenience, which is its polysemic character. An image conveys different meanings, which we are not always able to master. In the case of language, the phenomenon of polysemy is notably reduced by the context and the presence of other signs that guide the choice and understanding of reader or listener. The image, on the other hand, presents itself as whole and sole, not as a continuation of something else, and this is why it is difficult to determine its context. So what an image gains in impact it often loses in clarity. It should not be forgotten that communication is just one part of language. Language is also a means of conceptualization, a way of organizing the world, and thus is much more than mere communication. Animals, for example, communicate very well with both each other and human beings. What distinguishes the human from the animal is not communication but symbolization, i.e. the invention of non-analogical signs. At present the image is primarily part of the sphere of communication. It is repeatedly said that we've now entered the civilization of the image. But this is to overlook the fact that images are hardly ever used without words whether as caption, commentary, subtitle or dialogue."

Barbara Kruger,
Love for Sale, cover of the book
*The Words and Pictures
of Barbara Kruger*, 1990.

Graphics

Originally *graphein* meant both writing and painting. Consequently someone has divided the world, in a felicitous image, between those peoples who were "painters of ideographs" and those who were "singers of alphabets," first of all the Greeks, who eight centuries BC invented vowels and so, in essence, our own way of representing the sounds of language. Speech was shaped into something visible, sound was transformed into a figure; the world of primary orality (in which the fantastic process of humanization took place over tens of thousands of years) experienced the catastrophic shift from prehistory to history through writing. "The only historical event that coincided with the advent of writing was the foundation of cities and kingdoms, in other words the integration of a large number of individuals into a political system and their subdivision into castes and classes," Claude Lévi-Strauss points out in *Tristes Tropiques*.

"Writing, in reality, is inevitably always image," explains Giovanni Lussu. "The traditional contrast between writing and images turns out to be naïve: both are always images, structured in different ways and standing in different relationships with language. There are no absolute images with clear-cut meanings outside the way they are organized by language. Anthropological research, like research into iconology, shows that images, to be understood, have to be configured into systems of decodable signs. A good general definition of 'writing' is a 'system of decodable visual signs.' It follows that the so-called 'visual languages,' in order to be vehicles of unambiguously comprehensible meanings, must be 'scripts.' The much heralded culture of images may be nothing more than the culture of writing, freed from alphabetical prejudices."

And Roland Barthes comments: "The only systems of writing our scholars have studied thoroughly are ancient ones: the science of writing has only ever had one name, *paleography*, the precise, meticulous description of hieroglyphs or Greek and Latin letters, the skill of archeologists in deciphering ancient unknown scripts. But on our modern writing, nothing: paleography stops at the 16th century. Yet how could we fail to imagine that a whole historical sociology, a complex image of the relations that the classical human being had with his body, its laws, its origins, might emerge from such a *neography* that presently does not exist?... But what about the scripts of the 19th century? Or even those of our own century?"

**Display Scripts
and the Aesthetic
of Lettering**

"A script, any alphabetical composition used for exteriors, any script for display, in the broadest sense of the term, is no mere artistic expression using the forms of the alphabet or a vehicle for aesthetic values," Hermann Zapf explains. "It is, above all, a means of communication, for the simplest possible transmission of information. In addition to the printed alphabetic characters in books and newspapers, we come across compositions of letters of all kinds, by night and day, along roads and in cities. A bewildering jumble of signs confronts you when you enter any city nowadays. The whole world is united by this chaos, by this havoc wreaked on the landscape and on cities. Who is responsible for the visual pollution of our cities? At times it seems as if city administrations are run by the blind, or rather by visual illiterates. People who know how to read and write, of course, but who lack any feeling for the quality of signs and their use. This graphic pollution is planetwide, and identical in both East and West. So we need to make the people responsible for public works more aware of the importance of the quality of signage. In fact it is depressing to see how common poor-quality signs are in buildings. An architect should not limit himself to coming up with a beautiful design. He should also be concerned to integrate his new building into the environment. Careful study of signage in the building ought to be an integral part of the project. The ignorance revealed by the current poor quality of signs and inscriptions in public buildings is particularly irritating. In other times, the people with municipal responsibilities had a more educated taste and a feeling both for proportion and the design of lettering. Suffice it to recall, in this connection, the buildings of the Roman empire and baroque or colonial architecture. We have to get a debate going over public signs before it's too late. The problem at present is how to broaden the scope to cover the whole range of outdoor signs, which means not just in cities, but also in the landscape in general and, in short, the whole of our visual environment. Visual pollution is increasing daily, and replacing signs is an extremely burdensome task. At a time of growing awareness of the pollution of land and air, in an era of greater responsibility for the conservation of natural beauties, the ordinary citizen needs to be sensitized to the problem of visual pollution as well. A concrete proposal, to this end, would be to teach the art of writing from the very first years of schooling. There is no need for pupils to learn the refinements of calligraphy; they just have to be able to recognize the good and bad qualities of the design of lettering, and distinguish between good and bad proportions. In general, better education in the visual arts, in visual communication and in 'visible language' would allow us to halt the damage to the landscape caused by poor-quality signs. Education in the aesthetics of lettering is fundamental to instilling a sense of proportion and visual order."

Typology the characters of the visible word

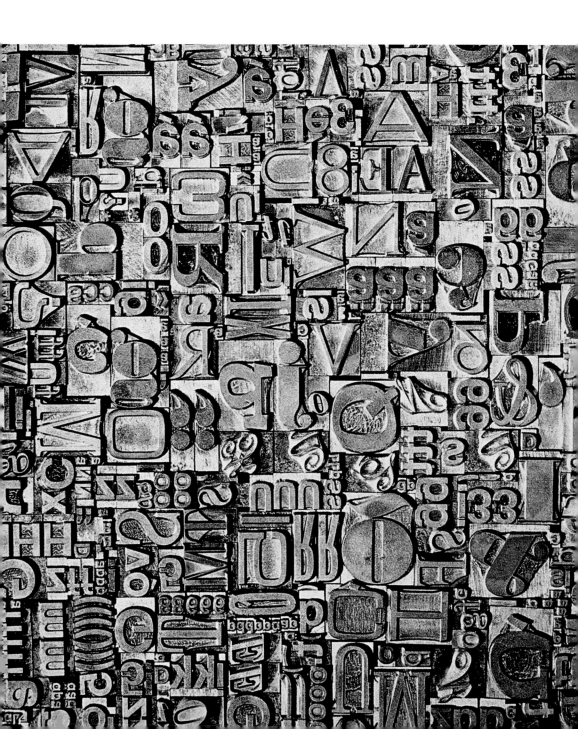

A case of coincidence of names: "typology" in the title is not the term so widely used in treatises of the 1700s and 1800s and the rich seam of architectural studies, and which has played a noteworthy role in theoretical writings on 20th-century architecture as well. Yet our "discourse on type" is also related to the Greek root *typos*. As Quatremère de Quincy explains in tome 3 (1825) of the *Encyclopédie Méthodique. Architecture*, the term *typos* "is used in a general sense, hence it can cover many degrees or varieties of the same idea. Consequently it may mean model, matrix, imprint, form, figure in high or low relief." This highly regarded author then points out that the term "is also applied to certain mechanical arts, as in the word *typography*."

The title of this entry refers to the technology of Gutenberg's print shop, the material medium of the many centuries of printing since the passing of the scribe, and calls attention to an essential part of its planning and process: the design of the "movable" characters of artificial script, the design of the "typefaces" of printed literature.

To begin with, it is necessary to recall that our "type" is made up of signs that stand for sounds: as such, it is derived from the letters of natural scripts, of alphabetical chirographies. In other words, it derives from systems for the manual notation of phonetic utterances, based on the representation of the components of the verbal sound fabric as separate particles. They are codified forms of communication, of language and therefore of thought, radically different in the economy of the medium and ease of circulation from the ideographic systems that preceded them in history and that are still in use over much of the globe. In fact writing originated about eight thousand years ago, when repeatable and recognizable graphic signs for the first time reified, isolated, fragmented, formed and rendered distinct the aural continuum of communication in pictograms (signs that represent ideas rather than sounds), conceptualized it in symbols and radically transformed the characteristics (highly conservative, formulaic and paratactic) of oral culture, which was the source of every form of human communication. Only much later, after a long process of development, was the sound fabric of the language represented in letters, in signs standing for sounds. This marked a break with the original figurative image of representable things/ideas to become a code that could be shared more widely. The extraordinary invention—if we can so describe it—of vowels, their transcription in letters, is a legacy of the Hellenic world, a few centuries before the Christian era, and the result of an atomistic perception of the phonetic structure of oral communication. In comparison with the far more complex earlier syllabic systems of the Middle East, the consequent extreme reduction of the number of alphabetic signs (to fewer than thirty) by the Greeks less than three thousand years ago finally made the sound of the word fully visible in an extraordinarily efficient, precise and economical way. This was to give rise to the Latin alphabet, still dominant in the West today.

Alphabets

Aa Bb Cc Dd Ee
Ff Gg Hh IiJj Kk
Ll Mm Nn Oo Pp
Qq Rr Ss Tt Uu
Vv Ww Xx Yy Zz

previous pages: photograph taken from the cover of a *Nebiolo* promotional leaflet, n.d.

Aa Bb Cc Dd Ee
Ff Gg Hh IiJj Kk
Ll Mm Nn Oo Pp
Qq Rr Ss Tt Uu
Vv Ww Xx Yy Zz

PostScripts

The acronym PDL (Page Description Language) identifies the software that is used in digital publishing to describe the page and its elements, including type. PDLs, unlike bitmaps, are resolution-independent: they update the page at the maximum resolution of the output device. The best known PDL is PostScript (a versatile general-purpose program, similar to Forth), written by John Warnock and partners and the source of the worldwide success of Adobe Systems, Inc., back in 1985. Sumner Stone has optimized the design of the PostScript family of typefaces, *Stone Sans*, *Serif* and *Informal* (1987), for printing within the limits of the 300 dpi of the early laser systems. Erik van Blokland and Just van Rossum have utilized a PostScript subroutine to create gradable random distortions in their Beowolf (1990).

The mature classical breakthrough of the alphabet took the form of a notational code of letters, establishing a convention of signs that were highly effective as a medium of communication and very simple to reproduce and learn, with remarkable typological stability in their form yet also subject to continuous morphological variations over time.

But there is more to it than this: all writing becomes visible, is materialized, is implemented only in so far as it becomes a physical sign. The impression of every letter is the result of the interaction of two vectors, applied to a code of configuration: the instrument that traces it and the surface on which it is traced. Depending on the nature of these two elements, alphabets—to put it very briefly—have developed and been transformed along a limited number of paths into two main categories: "archigraphies" and "calligraphies," to use two convenient labels. In the former we find the more ancient sense of the root of "-graphy," the Greek word *graphein*: to gouge, scrape, scratch, engrave—*sémata grápsas en pináki*, "he engraved the signs on the tablets," as the *Iliad* puts it. The chisel (any tool used to remove or cut into the material support, as in carving) has patiently been used to delineate in three dimensions the enormous range of inscriptions carved on pillars, stone tablets, friezes and classical monuments, the true talking books of antiquity and the favored sphere of the study of epigraphy. So on the one hand there is this "hard" tool that writes in relief (whether in positive or negative), making letters defined by contrasts of light and shade. This is archigraphy: letters engraved with careful deliberation one by one, where hesitation or error would be fatal; a durable script on a durable, essentially immobile support with a structurally stony character, closely bound up with the qualities of the supreme architectural material. The most obvious legacy of this in the multi-layered history of the alphabet, a complex artifact, is the repertory of what are commonly called "capital" or "uppercase" letters. The block capitals of Roman monuments, embellished in the Imperial era with terminal decorations known as "serifs," form one of the two basic components of our alphabet, which has retained an exceptional formal unity and coherence over many centuries and in many countries, obedient to strict requirements of perception as well as to fleeting elementary geometries, in virtue of a plastic sensitivity to light.

On the other hand, we have a "soft" instrument that writes by brushing the support and covering it with a layer, leaving a trickle, a slaver, a slime in its wake. "Calligraphy" is a two-dimensional tracing, stain, opacity: the tracing instrument (reed, quill, brush, nib and the like, implements also used by the painter) is a temporary store of dark, coating liquids. Instead of removing something from the surface, it adds a visible sign of its passage. The flat trace of the continuous movement of the hand, rather than the impact of an abrasion, covers a neutral, absorbent surface, making the letter a figure against a background.

Aa Bb Cc Dd Ee
Ff Gg Hh IiJj Kk
Ll Mm Nn Oo Pp
Qq Rr Ss Tt Uu
Uv Ww Xx Yy Zz

Aa Bb Cc Dd Ee
Ff Gg Hh IiJj Kk
Ll Mm Nn Oo Pp
Qq Rr Ss Tt Uu
Vv Ww Xx Yy Zz

Goodbye to bitmaps

Before PostScript, digital characters were described by more or less fine matrices of dots or, rather, pixels (picture elements): a sort of lattice, as in the needlework of the domestic science lesson our grandmothers used to get at school. When enlarged, the weave was revealed, with a typical serration, indentation or whatever you want to call it: in short, they pixellated! "*Modula* was the first PostScript typeface I designed," explain Zuzana Licko, *magistra litterarum* of *Émigré*, "with the Macintosh. In 1985, the computer was still very crude at drawing curves, but extraordinary for perfectly geometric typefaces. As a guide, I used the proportions of my Emperor 15 a bitmap." "The 45-degree diagonal, used for *Matrix* from 1986, again designed by Licko, "is the best that a laser can print."

So this form of writing enshrines the other pole of the etymon *graphein*: to paint, depict, represent. In it, the attractive and graceful strokes, the tactile sensuousness of the script, the fluidity of the lines, permit a more distinctive and personal expression. Generally continuous and flowing, "calligraphy" emphasizes speed of application, the figurative value of signs, the possibility of connecting them up into words and abbreviations; it is writing of relatively short duration, on ephemeral and essentially movable surfaces, structurally soft in character and closely bound up with the qualities of paper, the outstanding material for artistic drawing and its equivalents. So the subtractive power of "archigraphy" contrasts with the additive nature of "calligraphy," whose main legacy in the history of the alphabet is the family of letters we call "minuscule" or "lowercase," the final outcome of an age-old process of elaboration of the cursive or italic character, i.e. the non-monumental forms of classical script.

Gutenberg's movable type, by contrast, is made up of physical, tangible, manipulable and discrete objects: letters in relief on little blocks of cast lead, constitutionally isolated and separate from each other, true three-dimensional monograms (the observations of Giovanni Anceschi in *Monogrammi e figure* are of highly relevant here) set side by side, the wrong way round, to make up words, lines, columns and pages of text. Set in a galley, the page of lead is inked and its impression transferred by pressure to the paper, indenting it slightly and depositing the ink. This, in short, is the very durable technology that was handed down unaltered from the mid-1400s to the mid-1800s and survived almost to the present. The individual metal casts of the type were created with matrices that repeated the forms of the punches, the originals engraved (in series of different sizes, with suitable adjustments to allow for variations in the "body") by the designers of the letters or by skilled interpreters of other people's alphabetical signs. The history of typefaces is closely bound up with the architectural style and sensibility of an age, perhaps more so than any other art form, owing to the calibration of very subtle ratios and the implacable control of proportions that it demands.

For our purposes, which are not to describe the history of type but simply to identify the final, epoch-making breakthrough, it will suffice to point out a few basic factors. One was the contradictory initial state of affairs in which the first engravers of typefaces found themselves: they were trying to replicate, as finely as possible, the design, modeling and style of the superb calligraphic and polygrammatic qualities of the handwritten, chirographic letters of scribes, in short the age-old tradition of the past, but with a means that was intrinsically monogrammatic. A proof and consequence of this can be found in the extraordinary range of glyphs (imperceptible variants of the same letter that were combined in specific ways) of Humanist and Renaissance publishing, commencing with Aldine type (including

Type

Aa Bb Cc Dd Ee
Ff Gg Hh IiJj Kk
Ll Mm Nn Oo Pp
Qq Rr Ss Ttt Uu
Vv Ww Xx Yy Zz

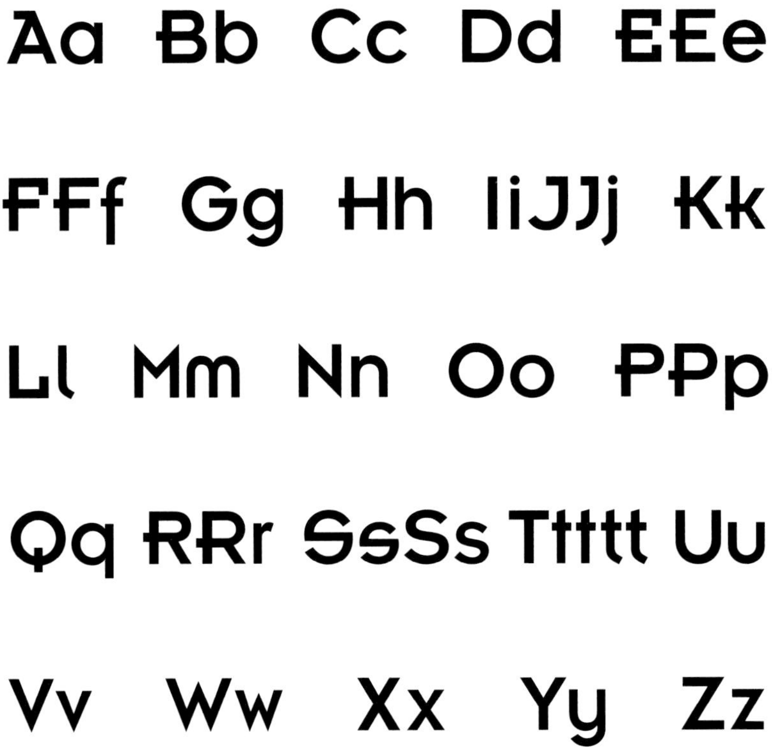

The great fame acquired by the Briton Neville Brody in the eighties was linked in part to the design of typefaces of a clearly "modernist" inspiration (with all the ambiguities the term implies): exemplary is the rigid elementary geometry of *Typeface Two*, conceived for *The Face* in 1984 (and then distributed under the name *Industria*), with which Brody intended to conjure up a thirties-style European rationalist "regime." Below, *Insignia* (1990), another of Brody's typefaces that is similar in conception.

Aa Bb Cc Dd EEe

FFf Gg Hh IiJJj Kk

Ll Mm Nn Oo PPp

Qq RRr SsSs Ttttt Uu

Vv Ww Xx Yy Zz

the invention of italics), and the subtle optical adjustments to match variations in the size of type found in the purest traditions of typography. Over the centuries these variations were discarded until they were nearly eliminated in the 1800s, gradually blunting a sophisticated and widespread sensitivity to visual balance in the typesetting of pages.

The second factor was the triumph of Italian Humanism in the design of type: the Renaissance imposed on the West the Latin alphabet, the rounded clarity of the *littera antiqua* (printing had emerged not long before with the bold and angular Gothic type used by Gutenberg); or rather, it was that original reinterpretation of classical antiquity that underlay the rebirth of the arts in Italy in the 1400s. The consequence was the definitive structuring of typefaces into two "cases," present in every complete Western alphabet: the archigraphic uppercase letters, the block capitals of Roman origin; and the calligraphic lowercase letters, the minuscule letters that had found their definitive form in the Carolingian Renaissance, nearly a thousand years later. To these we must add a multitude of non-alphabetical signs (from accents to punctuation marks) and numerals, which originated in India, were taken up by the Arabs and only came into widespread use in Europe in the 13th–14th centuries.

The third factor is the close bond between the tracing tool and the support in printing as well, between lead, ink and paper: a hybrid relationship, a "hard" instrument that hollows out the support to deposit a liquid trace, like the "soft" instruments; in short subtraction combined with addition.

Neography

The extreme stability of Gutenberg's technology meant that for centuries the design of typefaces evolved slowly but significantly through morphological variations in a direct, reciprocal relationship with these three factors. The closing decades of the 19th century altered and diverted the centuries-old tradition of patient research and slow improvements in type. The appearance of typesetting machines, such as Linotype and Monotype, took the place of the time-consuming manual preparation of the text. Combined with the spread of the pantograph, an instrument that speeded up the design of typefaces because a single model could be used for each size, it marked the beginning of a process of great simplification that was completed in the 20th century with the development and current dominance of offset and roto-offset printing. In essence, offset printing is a process in which ink is transferred by means of a cylindrical rubber pad from a plate engraved with the graphic elements of the page onto paper: the printing no longer indents the paper; the only pressure required is so much as is needed to make to the cylinder travel over the page. Thus the sheet of paper is painted, or rather smeared with ink: in short, this is a return to a "soft" instrument. In the second half of the 20th century, and at a breakneck pace since the mid-eighties, radical changes have also taken place

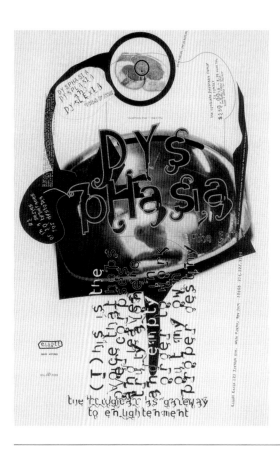

Examples of a tendency taken from nature itself, from the intimate complexion of the (the risky but perhaps necessary chances of experimenting with color, sound, movement, mutability and instability, already hinted at in van Blokland and van Rossum's *Beowolf*), the idiosyncratic, mutant and hyperactive typefaces of Elliott Peter Earls—which were a hit in Hollywood and have therefore been seen in the titles of films like *Spawn*—express the distinctive fusible verve and, at the same time, cruel destructive force of one of Cranbrook's most original alumni.

in the whole phase of preparation: the "hot-setting" of type is now part of industrial archaeology (and sometimes cause for nostalgia): first it was replaced by the "cold" processes of photocomposition and now it has been computerized. The digital typeface, materialized in positive on a plastic film, has eliminated the centuries-old lead. As early as the sixties, designers of letters found themselves facing uncertainties and problems comparable to those of the punchcutters of the Humanist period: first in their attempt to translate the historical legacy of tens of thousands of typefaces created for lead into "numerical" form, and then in confronting the critical question of the coherence between the system of tools and production and the design of letters.

The first digital letters were formed by an ever finer matrix of dots. The technology evolved rapidly (the PostScript page description language, the basis for today's pre-printing processes, emerged at the end of the eighties): the result is a scaleable geometric outline of the letters that reduces them to digital pantographs. A series of attempts (such as the MultiMaster types) have been made to remedy the poverty of type design inherited from the 19th century, but without much success. Desktop publishing, which potentially brings the formidable tools of digitally designed characters (can we still call them type?) within the reach of all, has at the same time launched a vigorous renaissance in lettering design all over the planet. It really boomed in the nineties, and not just in quantity. A new awareness of the ambiguous nature of digital type is spreading, with a more mature approach to the issues, after the often indigestible orgy of so much contemporary production, borne on a tide of greenhorn enthusiasm, transgressive excess and the insatiable demands of the market. Digital type has to respond, after all, to broader and more diversified needs than type designed for the printing press.

On the one hand, the evident success of the monitor, radically different from paper, as a new medium of communication, means there is a pressing need to design lettering for the screen, a need which some of today's most sensitive designers are trying to meet: on screen, letters can even change color, outline and position, as well as move around and emit sounds when needed. On the other, the transformation in the methods of printing on paper makes it necessary to take account of what is by now a universal division into two systems: low resolution (from the inkjet to the laser) in homes and offices; high resolution, with offset printing. And in these cases, too, the requirements for lettering design are quite different, owing to differences in the relationship between instrument and support. If we confine ourselves to high-quality printing, the burdensome legacy of the most conservative of the arts, typography, entails formal and conceptual prejudices that are difficult to set aside without more widespread critical attention to its problems and history on the part of all those working in the sector. And this is something that cannot take place without an understanding of the techniques

AAA BBB CCC DDD EEE

FFF GGG HHH IIIJJJ KKK

LLL MMM NNN OOO PPP

QQQ RRR SSS TTT UUU

VVV WWW XXX YYY ZZZ

AAA BBB CCC DDD EEE

FFF GGG HHH IIIJJJ KKK

LLL MMM NNN OOO PPP

QQQ RRR SSS TTT UUU

VVV WWW XXX YYY ZZZ

Digital calligraphy

Because of its elastic, penetrable nature (the complete opposite of the physical solidity of lead) the digital typeface appears to permit all kinds of experiments and revivals in the design of alphabets: deconstructively avant-garde, philologically conservative-reconstructive of the modern (in fact accurate historical versions of the ur-typefaces of Bayer, Bill, Renner, Tschichold, van Doesburg and the like have appeared), archaically ante-typographic (like the popular *Lithos* of Carol Twombly or the more charming *Herculanum* of the venerable *Adrian Frutiger*), nostalgically calligraphic, sagely epigraphic This last is the case with the many typefaces of Paul Shaw and Garret Boge: the Florentine set (1997) *Beata* (Bernardo Rossellino), *Donatello* and *Ghiberti*; the Roman baroque trio (1996) *Pontif*, *Pietra* and *Cresci*.

involved. To put it another way: are we told anything by the fact that Max Miedinger's ubiquitous Helvetica, dating from the mid-fifties, is simply an extremely popular but banal remake of the robust century-old Akzidenz Grotesk? Or that another excellent 20th-century character, Times New Roman, designed in the early thirties, is a true *pastiche*, constructed on Humanist axes, with Mannerist proportions, Baroque weights and a Neoclassical finish, as Robert Bringhurst has pointed out? To what extent is it legitimate to make digital versions of typefaces designed for manual typesetting, to be cast in lead and printed on a press, which leaves many fonts with the flavor of the "translators of the translators of Homer?" What does it mean, after the triumph of the instruments of design over the ideas of the first digital alphabets, *aprés le déluge* of a unique deconstruction, to observe an apparent return to order, with the redesign of fonts like Baskerville and Bodoni? Are the marked tendencies toward a revival of ligatures, glyphs and "calligraphic" figuration and the attempts at optical corrections of many of the most interesting contemporary digital fonts the only opportunities offered by digital technology, in the context of an intelligent "recovery" of the past, to "preserve" the heritage? Don't the radical researches of the modern era (with their geometric rigors, the dream of monoalphabets and similar experiments) also deserve careful reflection that looks beyond mere appearances? Might not the problem today be the same that has run through the entire history of writing, although rendered even more complex by the multiplicity of the tools now available: how to find an appropriate form rather than a "beautiful form," to establish a suitable coherence between the (digital) design of the letter, the tracing instrument and the support?

Among the many questions that still remain largely unanswered, in the eye of the digital "storm," one stands out, in conclusion, as a priority: hasn't the time come to equip ourselves with the means, both theoretical and operative, and with the methods that will allow us to come to grips with what we choose to call the science of modern and contemporary "neography?" In other words to give a disciplinary form to the study of shaping of letters into typographical and now digital forms?

Aa Bb Cc Dd Ee
Ff Gg Hh IiJj Kk
Ll Mm Nn Oo Pp
Qq Rr Ss Tt Uu
Vv Ww Xx Yy Zz

Aa Bb Cc Dd Ee
Ff Gg Hh IiJj Kk
Ll Mm Nn Oo Pp
Qq Rr Ss Tt Uu
Vv Ww Xx Yy Zz

Deconstructions

The new designers of digital typefaces have grown more implacable in their experimentation in recent years, producing excellent results through sadistic exercises of disassembly, abrasion, corrosion, découpage, frottage and collage, coupled with Frankensteinian transplants, perverse mutation and risky genetic hybridizations, under the banner of the death of history and the end of printing, seeking a deliberate "illegibility" combined with an impure "visibility" of the letters. Significant examples of all this: Barry Deck's *Template Gothic* (1990), critically inspired by the teaching of Ed Fella, in a sort of homage to the vernacular; *Dead History* (1990) by P. Scott Makela—another product of Cranbrook, like Fella himself—which, right from the name, is a whole program…

Aa Bb Cc Dd Ee

Ff Gg Hh Ii Jj Kk

Ll Mm Nn Oo Pp

Qq Rr Ss Tt Uu

Vv Ww Xx Yy Zz

Aa Bb Cc Dd Ee

Ff Gg Hh Ii Jj Kk

Ll Mm Nn Oo Pp

Qq Rr Ss Tt Uu

Vv Ww Xx Yy Zz

Reconstructions

"In the end a return of the 19th century has defeated our own century […] Let us be honest and call this what it is: an age of Restoration. But without Romanticism. Indeed, essentially neoclassical. An indecently futuristic neoclassicism," Mario Tronti has acutely observed. Something similar seems to have occurred in the world of typefaces recently: not coincidentally, Zuzana Licko, one of the most intelligent and sensitive figures on the scene, author of many of *Émigré*'s best-known, brand-new digital typefaces, has—and perhaps this is not such a great surprise—(re)designed her ideal Bodonian typeface with *Filosofia* (1996) ("before the age of personal computers … my favorite typeface was *Bodoni*") and the feminine *Mrs Eaves* (1996): "my first revival, based on the design of *Baskerville*."

paper architecture the graphics of stamps

The modern postal service was set up in the mid-19th century and acquired a central role in the systems of communication of nation states. This led rapidly to the constitution of specific administrative organizations and government agencies. Despite the unrelenting onslaught first of electrical technologies (from the telegraph to the fax) and then electronic ones (email above all), the postal service continues to play a major role in the distribution of both texts, or the word made visible through handwriting or printing, and pictures, a very widespread body of images that is in some ways highly specific (think of the saga of the illustrated postcard, with its heyday at the beginning of the 20th century). The emblem of this entire system of communication, the proof of payment for the service, is the postage stamp. The basic innovation here was economic: the cost (in the form of standard charges) of transmitting of the message was borne by the sender and not by the recipient.

The credit for this innovation is usually assigned to Sir Rowland Hill, a perfect example of progressive British pragmatism in the age of the unchecked spread of the Industrial Revolution. In the 1830s, the arguments advanced by Hill in his pamphlet *Post Office Reform: Its Importance and Practicability* met with rapid and efficient application under his direct supervision.

In September 1839, over 2,600 participants entered the design competition for the new graphic artifact, the postage stamp. Unhappy with the results, Hill decided to use his own version, a profile

1

2

3

4

5

of Queen Victoria taken from a medal. Known as the Penny Black, the world's first postage stamp was issued by the reformed British postal service on May 1, 1840, in a compact rectangular format (about 2 × 2.5 cm), thereafter long adopted as the de facto standard. In the 1840s and 1850s a growing number of countries, starting with the Swiss cantons of Zurich and Basel and Brazil, followed the British example. In the meantime the technical characteristics of the object were refined: format, design, paper, watermark, adhesive. To make the perforations (the first stamps were printed without perforations and had to be cut out with scissors), the Irishman Henry Archer sold the patent for the first perforating machine to the British government in 1854.

Over the space of one and a half centuries, once the standards and the conditions of international circulation had been established (the first international convention dates from 1874), the little paper rectangle proved an extraordinary worldwide success. It is probably one of the most significant documents of contemporary visual culture. A peculiar object of mass design, in the sense that it is one of the most common industrial graphic artifacts, the postage stamp (in addition to its economic function) is capable of conveying complex visual messages that often have a definite aesthetic content. At any rate, stamps are highly appreciated by the public. Proof of this popularity can be seen in the hobby of philately, one of the largest of all markets for collectors with an extensive specialized literature,

1 H.P. Berlage
Amsterdam Bourse
2 W.M. Dudok
Hilversum City Hall
3 G.C. Bremer
post office in The Hague
4 J.J.P. Oud
Shell offices in The Hague
5 Brinkman and van der Vlugt
Van Nelle factory in Rotterdam

6

7

8

9

though one that has only rarely interested art historians (Italy's Federico Zeri was one of the few exceptions). In this disregarded history, a role of particular importance was played by the PTT, the Dutch postal service, run by an exceptional director, Jean François van Royen. After condemning in no uncertain terms the limitations of the stamps produced by the state-owned enterprise in 1912 ("thrice horrible: horrible lettering, horrible composition, horrible paper; horrible the three main elements that define the aesthetic quality of printed matter"), van Royen succeeded in giving the post office a "visual identity" of the highest level over the next three decades. In fact he called upon the finest design talents in the country, turning to representatives of every discipline, including such architects and designers as K.P.C. de Bazel, M. de Klerk, P. Zwart and C.L. van der Vlugt. This contributed to the creation of a specific and extremely vital tradition of public design in the Netherlands, which extended from printed matter (and postage stamps in particular) to all the articles and products of the PTT.

The Dutch PTT's policy of "total quality" has continued down to the present day, even after its privatization, and has seen, over time, the involvement of such leading figures as W. Sandberg, D. Elffers, C. Oorthuys, O. Treuman, J. Swarte, J. Coenen and W. Crouwel. The case of the Netherlands, therefore, shows what can be achieved by a clear grasp of the value of postage stamps as a means of public communication together with a policy of commissioning designs

10

6 G. Rietveld
Schroeder House in Utrecht
7 R. van't Hoff
Henny Villa at Huis ter Heide
8 J. Duiker
school in Amsterdam
9 A. van Eyck
orphanage in Amsterdam
10 J.J.P. Oud
congress center in The Hague

from gifted professionals. But there are a number of other possible and interesting observations about the process of creation of the artifact in question.

By no means secondary is the choice of subject, the theme of the "commemorative stamp" (the majority of those in circulation), as collectors call any stamp that represents something more than its simple face value. Apart from children, philatelists today generally specialize in one subject or another (space exploration, flora, fauna, sport and so on). Yet readers will have great difficulty in finding thematic catalogues of stamps that depict works of architecture—very rare indeed—and still less of contemporary buildings. This absence reflects a peculiar and in its way significant contradiction, which ought to provide food for thought about the images that post offices project of their own countries, and especially of the present.

Architecture, in one way or another, is in fact one of the most common features of the images on postage stamps. But contemporary architecture barely gets a look in, reflecting a curious but not insignificant aspect of the culture of those who are responsible for making these choices, and above all of the image fostered by the State. We appreciate what is introduced into the common cultural heritage. In other words: everyone displays what he deserves. This appears, not without irony, to be what these anything but innocuous little paper rectangles tell us.

11 H. Hertzberger
school in Amsterdam
12 R. Koolhaas
theater in Scheveningen

11

12

left: *Campo grafico, "Review of the Ugly,"* inside page of issue 9, September 1933; analogously to postage stamps, the magazine of "graphic aesthetics and technique" tackled the theme of the institutional image by comparing streetcar tickets as they were and as they could be.

above: *Jolly Angelo Valaguzza,* cover of a promotional leaflet, 1960; a montage by Pino Tovaglia, made up of preprinted tickets.

talking figures the art of illustration

Despite the naysayers, the special activity of producing images known as "illustration" is still alive and in good health. It is passing through a phase of substantial renewal, creatively reinvigorated by an unsuspected capacity for change, an almost biological aptitude for cross-fertilization, for absorbing new influences without becoming nostalgic, for freely hybridizing compositional and figurative models and deliberately banal combinations of the means of expression (for example, with a disquieting and sophisticated neo-primitivism). These are all phenomena that—to continue our metaphor from the natural world—help to introduce a necessary variety into the members of the species, enriching its genetic heritage and preventing infertility.

But what is so peculiar, so specific about the sphere of graphic art we call "illustration," one is moved to ask, as we attempt to distinguish it amid the huge volume of images now being churned out and consumed voraciously, as never before, an aggressive process that seeks to prevent them from settling in the collective memory. In the sense in which the term is now commonly understood, illustration (in Paola Pallottino's precise definition) is the "printed reproduction of a graphic-pictorial work commissioned by the publishing industry and consequently found in its products" and always related to a text. It is part of the vast legitimate progeny of the industrial revolution in the field of imagery, or rather, of the technical reproducibility that is one of the results of that revolution, with an overwhelming impact on the arts.

It is no coincidence that the use of the term illustration in this sense first emerged in the birthplace of the industrial revolution, in Britain in the second decade of the 19th century, and then spread slowly through Europe. It was in the 1840s that the first periodicals systematically devoted to illustration (such as the *Illustrated News* in London and *Il Mondo Illustrato* in Turin) appeared, and it was then that the basic tradition was established, before the artistic genre was broadened to include other forms of publishing.

The modern meaning of illustration is a figure that explains or at least comments on a text: a figure that speaks or interprets. "To illustrate," however, has various other connotations and to get a clearer understanding of what we are talking about, it is worth pointing out that it means not only "to execute an illustration to commission," but also (a much older meaning) "to clarify, explain, elucidate." Once it also meant "to make illustrious," by direct connection with the Latin root *illustris*, and along the same lines we should remember that it originally had the sense of giving luster to something, i.e. adorning it, with consequent decorative, or even laudatory, implications, in keeping with its etymology. It suffices, for our purposes, to recognize at least intuitively how these meanings resound deep within the sense of "illustration" that we have accepted here.

Niccolò Tommaseo was already well aware of this over a century and a half ago. This is his comment: "The illustrations appended to the works of writers shed, or promise to shed, as much light on their words as serves to comprehend them or to give the reader pleasure in them." He goes on to say, with respect to illumination, that "illustration can be performed with the laborious means of human art."

So the ambiguous status of illustration lies in a dimension poised between heteronomy and autonomy, between subsidiarity to the words it is intended to clarify and its own intrinsic capacity for expression, which connects it with the ever wider field of the "arts of representation," in the modern sense of disciplines that aim at visual communication. So it is equally distinct from the complete autonomy of the work of art and the practical function of the technical drawing or plan, from the codified narrative synthesis of the comic strip and the essentially hyper-reproductive specialization of the digitally created image.

Understanding the incessant production of illustrations, though only by fragments, and forming provisional hypotheses, uprooting them from their immediate context but at the same time putting together comparable repertories, however summarily: this is the essential critical method for investigating their nature and identifying the characteristics that change with place and time, in short tracing their history. It is a complicated but unavoidable task if we are to understand, without apocalyptic anxieties or messianic expectations, the all-pervasive explosion of images that is such a distinctive feature of the contemporary era, conditioning every attempt to transform our culture.

the return of pictograms semiosis dresses up

For some time now, graphic designers have once again been taking an interest in pictograms, a special class of signs that fuse idea and image in an original and expressive amalgam that is highly effective as visual communication. Every so often it is useful to stop and get your ideas straight, to take another look at the definitions of the things you're writing about, so as not to get muddled or create confusion. There is a lot of talk about signs. But what is a sign? C.S. Peirce, one of the founders of semiotics (the general theory of signs and symbols and their function), explains in a celebrated passage that "a sign, or *representamen*, is something which stands to somebody for something in some respect or capacity. It addresses somebody, that is, creates in the mind of that person an equivalent sign." So the sign is a stand-in, a surrogate, a simulacrum of the object that it refers to, a conception that dates back at least to St. Augustine. "From this way of seeing," comments Ugo Volli, "derives the idea of an endless circulation of signs in social life, what Umberto Eco calls unlimited semiosis. So long as a phenomenon of communication, in particular a sign, remains alive, it goes on leaving new traces of itself."

But does that mean, one wonders, that signs are a language of communication? "In effect the term 'language' is often used metaphorically," argued Roland Barthes in an interview, "for any kind of communication or, and this is more serious, for any type of expression… Technically, 'language' is something very precise: in the system of signs that makes up our articulate speech, the signs are—if I can put it like this—divided twice: first into words, and then again into sounds (and letters). At the level of words, the relationship that unites signified and signifier is unmotivated. When we say 'ox,' for example, the sound itself has no analogical relationship with what we can call the 'mental image' of the ox. In fact the sound used changes from one language to another. The second articulation, that of the phonemes, functions by a finite number of oppositions, which are binary oppositions. For this reason it is said that our articulate speech is a digital code… Alongside our linguistic system of double articulation exist other systems of communication in which, this time, the relationship of signified and signifier is analogical. This is the case, for instance, with photography (in this particular case the relationship is very strong, very realistic, it could be said) and with schemes like those of road signs and certain drawings used for educational purposes. We cannot speak of 'language' in relation to signs without a double articulation, one in which the signifier/signified relationship is analogical... The image, as sign, as element in a system of communication, leaves a deep impression. Attempts have been made to study this shock value … but we need to be very cautious: as a sign, an image has one drawback, one considerable inconvenience, which is its polysemic character. An image conveys different meanings, which we are not always able to master... In the case of language, the phenomenon of polysemy is notably reduced by the context, the presence of other signs that guide the choice and understanding of reader or listener. The image, on the other hand, presents itself as whole and sole, not as a continuation of something else, and this is why it is difficult to determine its context. So what an image gains in impact it often loses in clarity… Yes, this *koiné*, this Vulgate of visual signs and symbols [to which the interviewer had referred in a question] common to all human beings can be very useful, but it can never be attained in this field, which has extremely restricted codes, as they are always analogical. And above all it should not be forgotten that communication is just a partial aspect of language. Language is also a means of conceptualization, a way of organizing the world, and thus is much more than mere communication. Animals, for example, communicate very well with both each other and human beings. What distinguishes the human from the animal is not communication but symbolization, i.e. the invention of non-analogical signs… At present the image is primarily part of the sphere of communication… It is repeatedly said that we've now entered the civilization of the image. But this is to overlook the fact that images are hardly ever used without words whether as caption, commentary, subtitle or dialogue."

This long citation from Barthes will have to satisfy us for the moment. Now we can go back to our pictograms with greater confidence. But not before turning to Tomás Maldonado to clarify another question of terminology: "The phonogram is a graphic sign whose referent is an element of expression of the phonological type. For example, the word 'stop' in traffic signals... The pictogram is an iconic sign whose referent is an object or a particular class of objects or again the particular quality or action that the class of objects may designate. For instance, the graphic representation of two children running to indicate 'school exit' in road signs... Finally, a diagram is a non-iconic graphic sign or one with a very low degree of iconicity. Usually the diagram is used to designate an event or a process or the way or place in which an event or a process occurs. In traffic signals, for instance, the triangle used to warn of a generic 'danger.'"

There is a growing need to find appropriate and sensible responses, neither repetitive nor banal, to precise requirements in the field of signage, which is increasingly common and in demand. Over the last decade this has led many renowned visual designers to take a second look at the classical repertories of pictograms, such as the ones used for public transport or to regulate traffic. With their roots in the pioneering efforts of the Italian Touring Club at the end of the 19th century, road signs later formed an important part of the "Viennese method" of Otto Neurath. This came to be known as Isotype, the International System of Typographic Picture Education, "a world language without words," developed for the representation of statistics. But all this is not enough to explain the peculiar attraction to pictograms evident in the personal researches of many contemporary graphic designers.

What such work reflects and richly underlines is not in fact the natural indicatory or prescriptive predisposition of these iconic signs, but an interstitial, residual aspect of pictograms, as analogical artifacts: their polysemy, their ability to produce new meaning, that stems from their constitutional ambiguity as images. This triggers a sort of unprecedented narrative synthesis, made up of paradoxical insights and terse statements (often poised between the apodictic and the caustic), obliging us to engage in a salutatory reflection on the nature of the signs that shape the imagery of contemporary graphics.

Men, pictograms, c. 1936;
designed by the Dutch designer
Gerd Arntz (1900–88)
for the Isotype system
of statistical representation
devised by Otto Neurath.

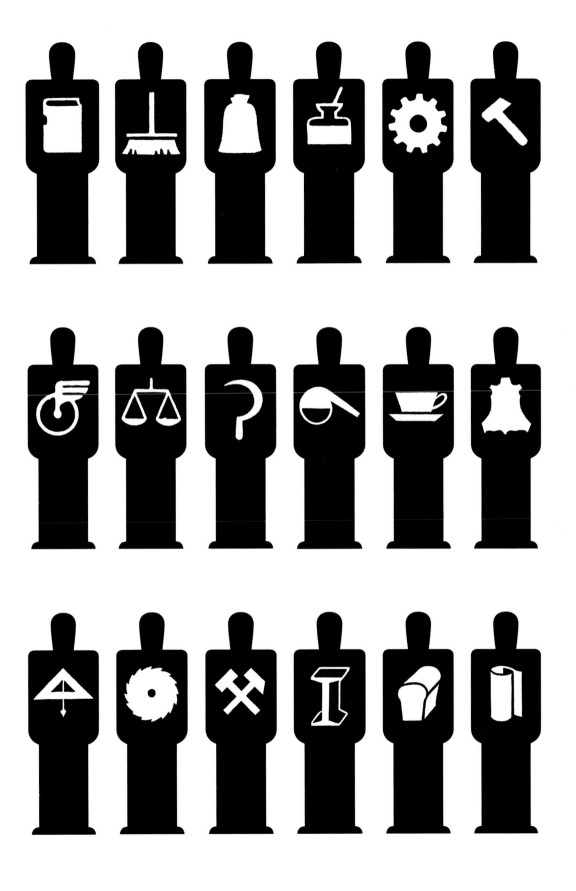

posters notes towards an imaginary entry in a history of visual thought

[General characteristics—define the concrete materiality of the object: the poster is a printed sheet of paper put up in a public place to convey information; hence it is a printed object without a verso, only a recto (a peculiarly one-dimensional character, like a photocopy); then speak of printing, and thus of pigments, inks and techniques, but also discuss the format, weight and nature of the different kinds of paper; refer to their sequential passage in time, i.e. history, between reproducibility of text and image. Stress the specific relationship between figure and ground (in the context of the street, the city, outside the city, the environment and so on) as well as the perceptual "distraction" that it entails (forms of vision and interpretations of space, i.e. relationship with architecture and the environment; reexamine, from this standpoint, the German literature of the late 19th-century: Schmarsow tactile mobile visual space; Hildebrand tactile-proximal vision, kinetic or dynamic Bewegungsvorstellung, optical-distant Fernbild; Raumscheu or *horror vacui* of Riegl and his friends); reflect on a printed form of mural art, in relation to the cultured as well as vernacular tradition of wall decoration (epigraphy, frescoes, stained-glass windows, murals) stressing the differences]

[History 1, forerunners, with caution and again stressing the differences; examples: *Acta diurna*; leaflets; imagerie d'Epinal; notices, announcements, edicts, proclamations and the like—history 2, excursus: political propaganda of the French Revolution; industrial revolution, merchandise and mercantile promotion (id est: advertising); the great French *affichistes* of the 19th century—Chéret, Daumier, Gavarni, Toulouse-Lautrec and the others—and lithography; spread of the poster and the late 19th century: Bernhard, Erdt and others in Germany, Beardsley and the Beggarstaff Bros. and others in the UK, Bradley and Penfield and others in the US, Italy eventually; between the wars: the influence of photography and painters (Braque, Chagall, Magritte, Matisse, Picasso, Man Ray, as well as de Chirico, Sironi and the rest), Bill in Switzerland, Carlu and Cassandre in France, Italy of course; postwar: Glaser, Kakemura, Matter, Müller-Brockmann, Savignac, Rand and others, don't forget the most recent ones and our own, plus Warhol and more recent artists]

In Italy the contemporary visual design of the "paper-on-the-wall" has its roots in a long tradition and in the fine reputation of the *cartellonisti*, the Italic equivalent of the Gallic *affichistes*.

or, more precisely, of the printed artifacts known as posters

[Investigate the etymology: *affiche* is linked to affix, from the Latin *ad-figere*, "to attach," formed out of the later participle—*fixus* instead of *fictus*, see fixed, fixture, interesting because it underlines the final immobility, the way it is stuck onto the two-dimensional plane of a wall (and is therefore a vertical figure), in contrast to other, movable and horizontal, forms of printed matter; the Italian *cartello*, originally *cartiglio*, meaning "cartouche" or "scroll," i.e. an inscription, the diminutive of the Latin *charta*, Greek *chartes*, "sheet of papyrus" and thus paper written on, cf. too the Spanish *cartél* and *cartilla*; *manifesto* is another Italian word meaning poster, from the Latin *manifestus*, "struck with the hand" then "caught red-handed," made up of *manus*—and a past participle *festus*, which we find in *infestus*, probably deriving from a desiderative form of the Indo-European root (one of the most important and fully documented) DHE "put" > "do," extended with—s, important for the twofold sense of manual character and surprise; poster meaning A: 1 a placard or bill posted or intended for posting in a public place, as for advertising; 2 one who posts bills, placards, etc. ("post" + "er"); but also poster meaning B: 1 see post horse; 2 (archaic) one who travels rapidly; hence see: to post; also *Plakat* (German) and *plakaat* (Dutch), as well as other languages]

[At this point images of recent posters ought to be inserted; for earlier ones, in other words for the history, a rigorous selection of real examples with all the necessary technical data (format, colors, printing, paper, etc., including collection, location, bibliography) and perhaps a visual-compositional analysis of each (not excessively pedantic nor academically didactic: difficult!); so look again at the following paragraph, before setting about new writing to order]

[Supplement the text here with various possible designers, but not too many]
The attempt to experiment with sophisticated iconic games, to play with the "message" and to tackle the intimate character of type (all performances critically mindful [at their own peril] of the unrepeatable achievement of the historical avant-garde movements in the first half of the 20th century) is a contemporary trend in posters that reveals an evident passion for the contemporaneity of the apparently out-of-date: the "arrière-garde looking to the future"; a fascination with the history of communicative artifacts as a source of visual culture.

To the cultivated eye, to votaries, perhaps even to dilettantes who still take delight in the art of the print, the faint echoes that can be heard in the posters of these designers, the quiet, conceptual references to the traditions of the craft, will in fact be transparent (and so invisible, as befits any good aid to demonstration; and they are not the only ones in need of a naturalness of artifice).

Like the predilection for concentrating the poster into a single, eloquent figure (*vel per imago vel per verbum*), usually against a ground of "non-color" (as good old van Doesburg, the theorist of De Stijl's chromoplastic, would have defined it): little color, and only where it's needed, if at all. Like the repeated use of visual metaphors and figurative games (witty images, rather than witty words), linked to a layer of double, or rather secondary interpretation (aberrant decoding vs. production of text?), subsequent to the "immediate" message (non-mediated, primary decoding: surface coding).

Like the work done on type (in the 20th century mostly "objective," and some of moderate inventiveness) and its sorting into lines, columns, boxes, squares, lumps and spots to form figures on figures, within a given figure, i.e. in a rectangle, usually with its longest side up and proportions of $1:\sqrt{2}$. (In this connection, why not reread Tschichold's "Die Proportionen des Buches," in *Der Druckspiegel* [Stuttgart], January–March 1955?). Or like certain free-style humorous or openly calligrammatic components, in a reshuffling of historical debris typical of our late culture, whether we characterize it in terms of excrement, slag, residue, neo-barbarism or the finest neo-medievalism (Apollinaire + Malevich + Mondrian, for example). Like the wandering of visual vectors in the plane, with points of application that do not coincide and are thus caught up in a cobweb of structural tensions that run through the construction of the sheet, coagulating in a kinetically unstable equilibrium. Like the unconcealed admiration for the elementarist typo-photo style of the twenties/thirties and other celebrated trends in visual thinking between the wars. Like the limited repertoire of basic geometrical forms (what shall we call them? Platonic solids) and the emulsion of materials.

Above all, like the open supremacy of the idea (etymologically: *idéin*—to see, appear, know; thus: to constitute in progress, through mental vision, as cognitive/design phenomenon), sometimes in a conceptually baroque manner, with respect to the material, physical crystallization of a form in the substance of the poster.

[Here other observations on the role of the Bildhafte Denken and of history (seen as current knowledge through first-hand study of the artifacts in question) as inspiring muse would not be out of place. Copy, if you want to understand—copy, if you want to take in, digest, metabolize, expel. One could elucidate some cheerfully apocalyptic and frivolously gossipy commentators on the "end of the poster" and the "inconveniences of memory," pointing out that yes, perhaps we are seeing the twilight of the poster, marginalized by the new media. So writing about this artifact is an exercise in nostalgia at the best of times; but perhaps it is also true that in the history of artifacts of communication what happens is not what happens with money (where the new drives out the old), but what our Gattopardo was well aware of, that everything changes and nothing changes. In other words the different media overlap, on different levels without canceling each other out, and they are all powerfully transformed together whenever there is some profound evolution/revolution (like the digital one). Today the poster is certainly no longer gloriously triumphant as at the turn century; nor is it at all like the modernist and highly effective *sachlich* poster of the years between the wars and immediately after, but something quite new, much as the book is and will increasingly be in relation to "multimedia"].

[Long live the poster, in any case. Today we find it, without too much surprise, the only "medium" that is growing rapidly, both in the national sector of business advertising and at the height of an Italian electoral campaign that resembled the referendum on kingdom vs. republic back in 1946 (*mutatis mutandis, si parva licet*). The election was fought out against a background of intensive bill-posting, in urban environments (including all the rail stations) and on highways, with blown-up photocopied mug shots, horrible party logos and backgrounds in boorish colors, with placards and totems and posters, all of them utterly hideous and disappointing in their design (for everybody, except the admen on the opposing sides, party leaders and their retinues, clearly averse to any image not of the promotional-marketing type). Allow me, those few readers who have had the patience to remain with me thus far, to finally vent my (civic, cultural and perhaps even political) spleen: as if we did not have, in this fine country of ours (as we have always had, from the end of the 19th century onward), good designers of posters, whether for the streets or elsewhere... It's a long, long road; anyway, *habent sua fata libelli*, so our fathers taught us].

digital soup culture of the cd-rom?

Digital soup is the primordial broth of contemporary culture, the stew, the rehash of a radical transformation of the modes of preserving, transmitting and producing knowledge in the great cauldron of human communication. We want to know more, we aspire to have a better idea of what's boiling in the pot, from those who are skillfully cooking this soup, preparing the ingredients and experimenting with flavors in tasty dishes to test special new recipes for CD-ROMs. Here is a brief introductory outline or picture (certainly not the only one) in which we can set the appearance, the spread of the digital; a hint, a glance through the lens of history, which is always obliged to look back from the present, to explore the significance of what is now happening. In talking about the present, many people describe it as "sur-modern": an age of excess and dispersion, with the acceleration of time and the contraction of space, a loss of the frames of reference in which bodies of knowledge and practices once used to be set.

Today we are, in other words, faced with an extraordinary confusion: cultural con-fusion, in the strict and deepest sense of fusing together, blending, hybridizing, crossbreeding, transfusing and transmigrating, whose course and direction are as yet unknown, which we fail to grasp fully but which we see at work, day by day, in every field of human activity.

It is not, however, simply a question of technology. It is not the advent of the digital, foreseen or unforeseen, that creates these apocalyptic concerns or messianic expectations. What interests us here are the effects of a new technology already in existence, or at least so advanced and extensive as to leave little room for doubt about its burgeoning, inescapable pervasiveness and invasiveness. A rehash I called it: because it amount to the preservation, transmission and production of human knowledge, and therefore nothing new.

It is now widely believed, and not just in scientific circles, that the means of communication, the media through which human beings communicate, directly influence the way in which they think. In other words, they define the characteristics of human societies, which—as Marshall McLuhan put it—"have always been shaped more by the nature of the media by which human beings communicate than by the content of the communication." If this is true, to understand the digital, i.e. the present, it may be useful for us to look back at the epoch-making changes in communication that came before it. Obviously we shall have to omit the problem of the origins or development of language, the organized emission of meaningful articulate sounds in speech and thus the question of oral cultures. (This is hard for us even to imagine, accustomed as we are to the word made visible and reproducible: a time when listening was the center, the source of knowledge.) We should always remember there have actually been very few great historic innovations in the technology of human communication. There was the introduction of writing six thousand years ago, in the 4th millennium BC (chirographic culture), which according to Ong, "transformed human consciousness ... more than any other single invention"; printing in the middle of the 15th century (typographic culture), still the dominant form that we are accustomed to mentally; and now just five hundred years old; the electric/electronic communication of the recent past, from the telegraph to radio and television, all technologies based on analog, material, physical and atomic media (to use Negroponte's words). To these we now have to add the discontinuity, the rupture of digital communication, which is embodied, made visible, on the computer and the monitor. Digital communication is based on the relative immateriality of "bits," on the extreme reduction of the complexities of communication/information to an elementary duality (1/0, on/off, to put it briefly). Yet it definitely seems capable of conveying greater complexities of communication/information by superimposing layers, interfaces, operations that translate these elementary binary states into structured flows for human comprehension, generating quantitatively and qualitatively powerful interrelations of unprecedented, unknown dimensions, still largely unexplored. This stratified and increasingly rapid succession of media, of instruments of communication, makes it possible to circulate information—at ever greater speeds and lower costs—to the point of excess and with the fertile, overflowing dissipation (a problem in itself) of our confused sur-modernity.

To conclude, here is a far-fetched but useful comparison. At bottom, it is as if we were living sometime around 1460. Gutenberg had produced the first printed book about five years before. He didn't know what he was doing from our point of view: i.e. that he was changing the human way of thinking, altering the modes of preservation, transmission and production of knowledge. He couldn't know it: this is the common destiny of new media (the radio was meant to be used for speech, but has ended up broadcasting music; and the fate of the telephone was quite different from what its inventors intended). Gutenberg was looking for a way to produce writing artificially; he wanted to improve, to optimize what he was familiar with, his historical legacy: handwriting. Instead, his artificial writing was to define the whole of Western culture and its dominance of the planet over the last five centuries. CDs were invented to store sound, music, and then turned out to be a highly flexible medium, well-suited to digital communication in all its forms. So are CD-ROMs just a mode of distribution, a sort of dry run for some far broader interactive device operating via the monitor, or do they foreshadow a new, creatively fascinating and necessarily little explored path of culture, to which we are as yet unable to give a name?

Study for cover, photograph by Grit Kallin-Fisher, 1930; in this image, the analogical instruments of the graphic designer.

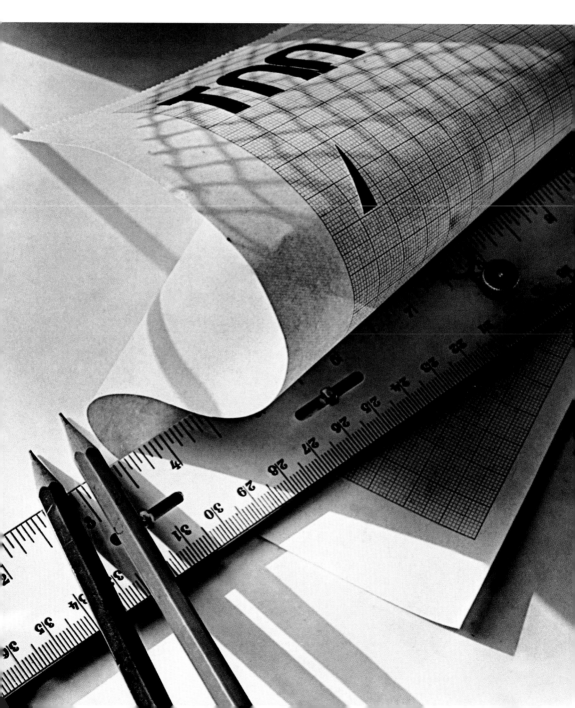

peter behrens zeitgeist and letters

Born in 1868, Behrens lost both parents when he was fourteen. Inheriting a substantial fortune, he decided to become an artist, studying first in Hamburg, then Karlsruhe and Düsseldorf and finally Munich, a very active cultural center in Germany at the time. From the social realism of the paintings of the early nineties, Behrens turned to Symbolism for inspiration, and then to the Jugendstil. He also designed objects for everyday use: porcelain, glassware and furniture.

His work in the applied arts earned him a prominent role in the Künstlerkolonie founded at Darmstadt by Grand Duke Ernst Ludwig von Hessen to "fuse art and life": in 1899 he was invited to be one of the seven members of the "artists' colony." It was in 1899 that he first tried his hand at lettering: he designed decorative running headlines for *Deutsche Kunst und Dekoration*. Deeply involved in the contemporary debate on art, technology and society, Behrens was convinced that, after architecture, typography "provided the most characteristic image of an age and the strongest evidence of its spiritual progress." To demonstrate this, he wrote, paged and illustrated his first important essay, *Feste des Lebens und der Kunst* (1900), with scrupulous attention to its visual effect. Probably for the first time in the history of typography, the running text was composed in a sans-serif font, which was to become established as the typical typeface of the modern era in the following decades. He took a similar approach to the cover of *Dokumenten des Modernen Kunstgewerbes* (1901), for which he designed an alphabet without serifs, modeled on the square.

The problem of typographic reform and the design of font was, in fact, one of the questions which most engaged Behrens's attention at the beginning of the 20th century. His aim was to "find a new typeface, in keeping with contemporary sensibility and style, simple and legible," because "we need a character of serious style for serious books: only then will we be able to transfer this noble style into daily life."

In 1901–02 he came up with his first printed font, produced by the foundry of the Klingspor brothers, the Behrens-Schrift (very similar to its author's neat handwriting): a severe and tight typeface, it was an attempt at a fusion between Gothic and Latin. Fritz Ehmcke compared it to a steel frame. In his presentation of the lettering, *Von der Entwicklung der Schrift*, Behrens explained that "a new character can be developed only in an organic and almost imperceptible manner from tradition, only in harmony with the new spiritual and material contents of the entire age" and that reading a text is like "observing the flight of a bird or the galloping of a horse: phenomena that appear graceful and pleasing even if the eye is unable to distinguish the details of their forms and movements; the observer sees only the rhythm of the lines. The same is true of a character."

In 1903 Behrens moved to Düsseldorf to became director of the arts and crafts school. From 1904 onward his work came under the influence of the systematic aesthetics of Dutch design, especially that of J.L.M. Lauweriks, whom he persuaded to come and teach in Düsseldorf (after hoping to get hold of H.P. Berlage).

left: Peter Behrens (Hamburg 1868, Berlin 1940); the photograph shows him sitting in front of the model for the *Competition for the New Layout of Alexanderplatz*, 1928–29.
below: the evolution of the design of the *AEG* logotype; Franz Schwechten, 1896; Peter Behrens, 1908; Peter Behrens, c. 1912.

In 1906–07 Behrens ran two courses in lettering and typography at Düsseldorf, with the assistance of Fritz Ehmcke and Anna Simons (the pupil of the greatest calligrapher of the 20th century, Edward Johnston, whom Behrens had also tried to get as a teacher). It was with her that Behrens designed the inscription "Dem Deutschen Volk" in 1909, only placed on Paul Wallot's Reichstag in 1917 after much controversy. His second typeface, the elegant and fluid Behrens-Kursiv, was produced by Klingspor in 1906–07.

1907, the year the Werkbund was founded. It marked a fundamental turning point in Behrens's career: he was appointed artistic adviser to AEG. In this role, the work he did was of enormous significance and quite without precedent. He designed the company's buildings, products and communications, in an attempt to create a higher synthesis of neoclassicism and *Sachlichkeit*: the hexagonal trademark (1907), applied everywhere; the graphics for publications of extreme refinement, such as the catalogue for the Deutsche Schiffbau-Ausstellung (1908) and the company "Mitteilungen" (from 1908). And then there was the Behrens-Antiqua typeface (1908), produced by Klingspor for exclusive use by AEG from the outset and inspired by the classical proportions of antique lettering, with a monumental character and uncial variations.

The geometric decorations that he designed for the Kursiv and Antiqua typefaces, on the other hand, were clearly derived from Alois Riegl's masterpiece *Die Spätrömische Kunstindustrie* (1901). Behrens's last set of characters produced by Klingspor, the Behrens-Mediäval, appeared in 1914 (the same year as the Werkbund exhibition in Cologne, for which Behrens also designed a splendid poster): conceived in 1906–07 and developed over the years 1909–13, it is a typeface of Renaissance inspiration, with a few idiosyncrasies in the serifs.

However, this was not Behrens's last font: his precocious appreciation of type without serifs, utilized on several occasions, led him to design a sophisticated sans-serif for AEG, in singular coincidence and harmony with a famous prototype of 20th-century typography, the Underground sans-serif that Edwards Johnson designed for the London subway, still in use today.

**Lettering and vignettes
on covers executed with
Behrens-Kursiv, in a specimen
designed by Peter Behrens
for the Klingspor foundry, 1907.**

Voyage au centre de la terre par Verne

Fahrplan der Rigibahn

Tagebuch

Esther par Racine

Dom Schlechten kann man nie zu wenig und das Gute nie
zu oft lefen: fchlechte Bücher find intellektuelles Gift, fie
verderben den Geift. Um das Gute zu lefen, ift eine Be=

*Vom Schlechten kann man nie zu wenig und das Gute nie
zu oft lefen: fchlechte Bücher find intellektuelles Gift, fie verderben den Geift. Um das Gute zu lefen, ift eine Bedingung,*

Vom Schlechten kann man nie zu wenig und das Gute nie
zu oft lefen: fchlechte Bücher find intellektuelles Gift, fie
verderben den Geift. Um das Gute zu lefen, ift eine Be-

Vom Schlechten kann man nie zu wenig und das Gute
nie zu oft lefen: fchlechte Bücher find intellektuelles Gift,
fie verderben den Geift. Um das Gute zu lefen, ift eine

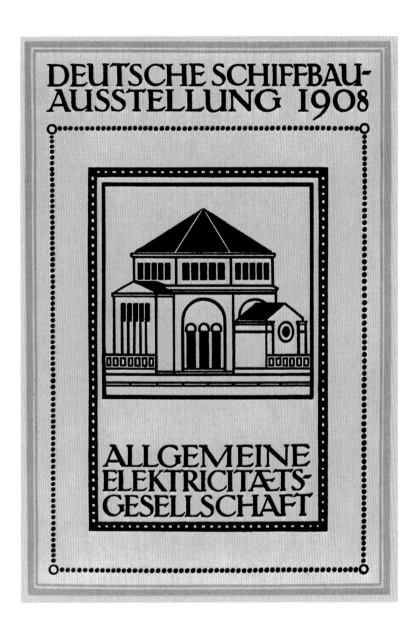

left: the main typefaces designed
by Peter Behrens, who created
Behrens-Antiqua for the exclusive
use of *AEG* in 1908.
above: *AEG the German
Shipbuilding Industry*, cover
of the brochure for the exhibition,
1908.

below: cover of the specimen
book of the *Behrens-Antiqua*
typeface, 1908.

above: *AEG Manufactures Arc Lamps*,
catalogue cover, 1908.
facing page: *AEG Intensive Arc
Lamps*, advertisement, 1911;
AEG Tachometer, advertisement,
1908.
top and bottom right: names of
months, typeface study, reproduction
of the original pen-and-ink drawings,
c. 1908.

FEBRUAR

MÄRZ MAI

JUNI APRIL

JULI AUGUST

SEPTEMBER

OKTOBER

NOVEMBER

DEZEMBER

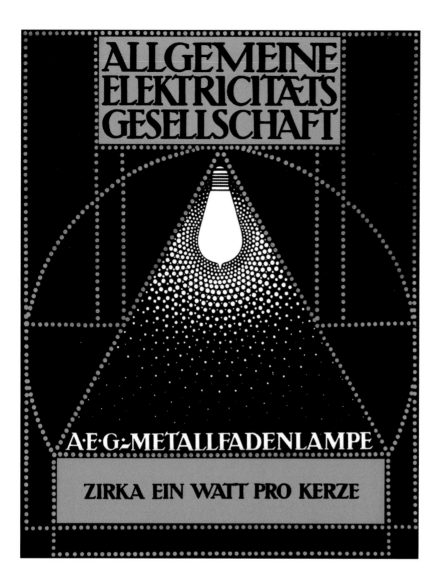

AEG Metal Filament Lamp,
poster, 1907.

el lissitzky the electro-library of the constructor

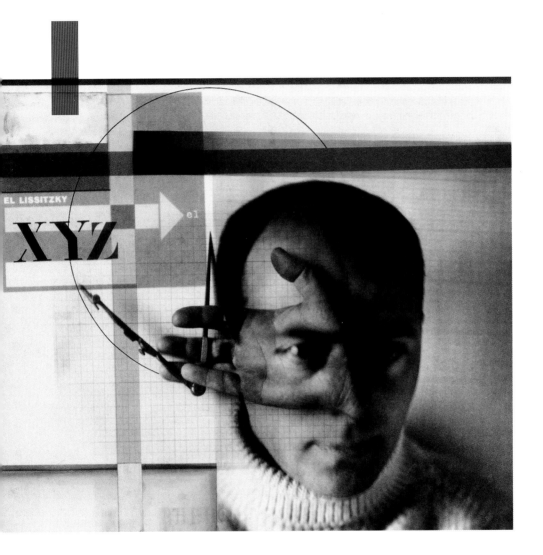

"Every invention in the field of art is unique. It has no follow-up," wrote El Lissitzky in the *Gutenberg-Jahrbuch* of 1926–27, in an essay entitled "The New Book." "Around the invention, over the course of time, various variations evolve on the same theme. Sometimes they are more discerning, sometimes more pedestrian, but rarely do they attain the force of the original. So it goes on, until the action of the work of art, by long use, becomes automatic and mechanical: the time is ripe for a new invention... Gutenberg, inventor of the system of movable type, used it to print many volumes that are true masterpieces of the art of book. Then came several centuries without fundamental inventions in our field (until photography)... It is shortsighted to think that only the machine, i.e. the replacement of manual processes by mechanical processes, is important in altering the appearance and forms of things. In the first place, the change is determined by the public with its requirements... Nowadays this no longer means a restricted circle, but 'everyone,' the masses. The idea that moves the masses today is called materialism but what characterizes the age is dematerialization... The material is reduced, we dematerialize, we replace inert masses of material with live energies. This is the sign of our times... So long as the book necessarily remains a tangible object ... we can expect, day by day, new and fundamental inventions in its production, to bring it up to the level of our age too. There are signs that this fundamental invention is going to come from the field of phototypesetting. This is a machine that transfers the typesetting onto a film and a printing press that reproduces the negative of the composition on sensitive paper. In this way the enormous weight of the typesetting material and the can of ink disappear, and so here too we have dematerialization. The most important fact is that the production of words and images is subjected to a single process: phototypesetting, photography. This photography still constitutes the type of representation that offers the maximum of comprehensibility to all. Thus we are faced with a form of the book in which representation becomes primary and the letters of the alphabet secondary... Hence I believe that the future form of the book will be representative-plastic."

I have a deep-rooted distrust of prophesies and the people who make them; otherwise I would feel justified in describing this passage by El Lissitzky as "prophetic."

It is undeniable that some of his general philosophical considerations (on the non-evolutionary uniqueness of "inventions" or the role of dematerialization, for instance) were accurate, and that his sensitivity to new developments in visual communication (the subject of these columns) was timely. El Lissitzky seems to have both anticipated the reduction/standardization of words and images to a single medium that we are seeing today, and realized the significance of a process that was then in its early days with the Uhertype phototypesetter, i.e. the passage from the preparation of text by hot-metal casting to the cold technique of photocomposition used in publishing.

left: *The Constructor*, photographic self-portrait of El Lissitzky (Lazar Markovich Lisitsky, Pochinok 1890, Moscow 1941), 1924. below: the logotype mark—visible in the self-portrait, on the left underneath the spatial coordinates xyz—that El Lissitzky used for his personal letter paper.

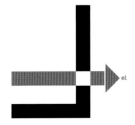

But to get a clearer understanding of the merits and contradictions of the contribution made by the extraordinary Russian "Constructivist" to 20th-century graphics, one can hardly do better than read the penetrating portrait of him by Jan Tschichold (another outstanding figure in the history of visual design) in the pages of the Swiss *Typographische Mittelungen* in 1965: "El Lissitzky, one of the great champions of typography in our technical age, was a man of sparkling intelligence and lively gestures, slim, fairly small in stature and, in his own way, almost a dandy, but serious-minded. His impulse to create was irrepressible and, even when in company, he always had to be doing something: taking photographs, drawing, writing. The fact that he had studied engineering at the polytechnic in Düsseldorf from 1909 to 1914 redounded wholly to the advantage of his creativity, which was expressed in a unique way. For him, every problem was fundamentally technical. But his intellect often took flight with his imagination, which came up with ideas even before being steered in a particular direction. He saw himself as an engineer, and was an artist... As a typographer, El Lissitzky ... had to work with the lead typesetting of Gutenberg, invented almost five hundred years earlier, little suited to his world of form and too heavy for it. The experts immediately pointed out the technical flaws and drawbacks of his diagonal composition. El Lissitzky did not develop his forms on the basis of the technique of typesetting... All the rest, however new and potent, often reflected the difficult struggle of the amateur typographer with an old and balky technique of printing... The force of many of his compositions stemmed from a protest against the monotonous drabness that he found in all printed matter... With nonchalance he set large titles and broad stripes on the page, imparting order to the whole and placing the accent on one point, to jolt the reader... It was a question of jolting the reader and not pleasing him, even in the typographical presentation of a text... He looked at too many things, perhaps he had too many ideas. This prevented him from devoting himself totally to a problem. However powerful the impact of his typography, it was sometimes wanting in the details. His typographical compositions anticipated, as we can see today, the possibilities offered by phototypesetting on film, which would have allowed him to do everything that he had in mind."

As early as 1923, in fact, in an article entitled "Topography of Typography" published in *Merz*, El Lissitzky had proclaimed: "The printed sheet overcomes space and time. The printed sheet, the infinity of the book, has to be surpassed. THE ELECTRO-LIBRARY."

K UNST

1924

ISM

1914

FILM US
KONSTRUKTIV US
VER US
PROUN US
KOMPRESSION US
MERZ US
NEOPLASTIZ US
PUR US
DADA US
SIMULTAN US
SUPREMAT US
METAPHYSIK US
ABSTRAKTIV US
KUB US
FUTUR US
EXPRESSION US

For the Voice, book
by Vladimir Mayakovsky
designed by El Lissitzky, 1922;
"this book of poems …
is intended for reading aloud.
I have made it an index book
to spare the reader the need
to search for individual poems.
This book is made up solely
of material from the type case.
Exploiting the possibilities
of two-color printing
(superimpositions, cross
hatchings and so on), …
I wanted to create an equivalent
unity between poetry
and typographic elements."

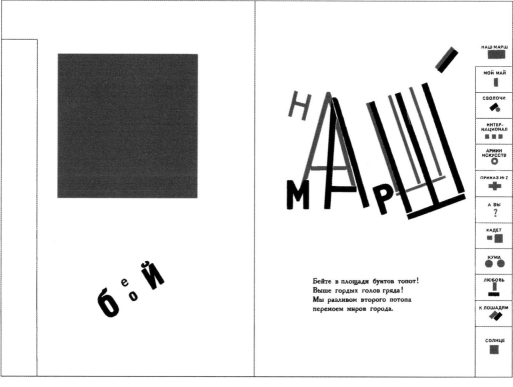

cover / our march

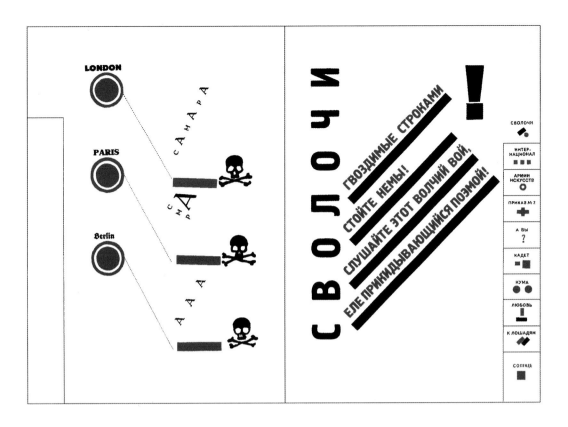

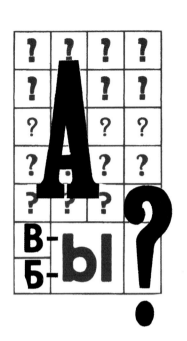

а вы могли бы?

Я сразу смазал карту будня,
плеснувши краску из стакана.
Я показал на блюде студня
косые скулы океана.
На чешуе жестяной рыбы
прочел я зовы новых губ.
А вы
ноктюрн сыграть
могли бы
на флейте водосточных труб?

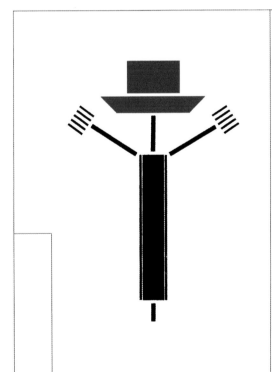

СКАЗКА о КРАСНОЙ ШАПОЧКЕ

• • •

Жил да был на свете кадет,
В красную шапочку кадет был одет.
Кроме этой шапочки, доставшейся кадету,
ни черта в нем красного не было и нету.
Услышит кадет — революция где-то
шапочка сейчас-же на голове кадета.
Жили припеваючи за кадетом кадет
и отец кадета, и кадетов дед.

Поднялся однажды пребольшущий ветер —
в клочья шапченку изорвал на кадете.

И остался он черный, а видевшие это,
волки революции сцапали кадета.

Известно какая у волков диэта:
вместе с манжетами сожрали кадета.

Когда будете делать политику, дети,
не забудьте сказочку об этом кадете.

ВОЕННО-МОРСКАЯ

ЛЮБОВЬ

По морям, играя носится
с миноносцем миноносица.

Льнет, как будто к меду осочка
к миноносцу миноносочка.

И конца-б не довелось ему
благодушью миноносьему.

Вдруг прожектор, вздев на нос очки,
впился в спину миноносочки.

Как взревет медноголосина:
„Р-р-р-астакая миноносина."!

Прямо-ль, влево-ль, вправо-ль броситься,
а сбежала миноносица.

Но ударить удалось ему
по ребру по миноносьему.

Плачь и вой морями носится:
овдовела миноносица.

И чего это несносен нам
Мир в семействе миноносином!

ЛЮБОВЬ

К ЛОШАДЯМ

СОЛНЦЕ

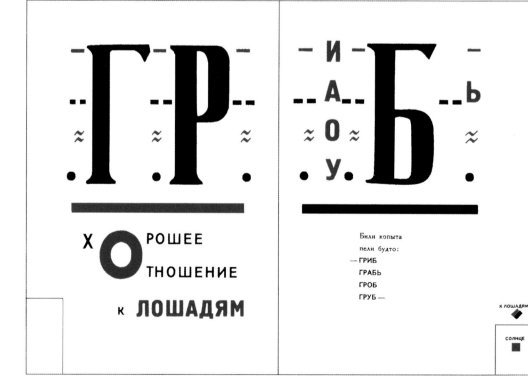

ГРИБ

ХОрошее Отношение к ЛОШАДЯМ

Били копыта
пели будто:
— ГРИБ
ГРАБЬ
ГРОБ
ГРУБ —

К ЛОШАДЯМ

СОЛНЦЕ

НЕОБЫЧА ЙНЕЙШЕЕ

БЫВШЕЕ
СО МНОЙ

ПРИКЛЮЧЕНИ

С

ВЛАДИМИРО МАЯКОВСКИ М

П

НА ДАЧЕ РУМЯНЦЕВА, ПУШКИНО, АКУЛОВА ГОРА.
ЯРОСЛАВСКАЯ Ж. Д.

солнце

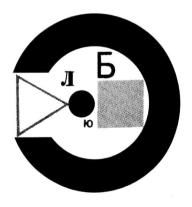

alexander rodchenko advertising-constructor

Alexander Mikhailovich Rodchenko was born in St. Petersburg in 1891 and died in Moscow in 1956. He holds an eminent position in that array of versatile artists and designers in the USSR who displayed their extraordinary creative powers in the twenties and early thirties, under the banner of Constructivism and its significant variants, in the "dream of a long prospect of dissent," as Alberto Asor Rosa suggested some time ago.

Tirelessly active in the fields of painting, photography, cinema, theater and the design of articles of everyday use, clothes and artifacts of communication (the specific reason why we are looking at him here, in a sort of follow-up to the text on El Lissitzky), in that period Rodchenko was contending with the immediate consequences and blatant contradictions of the Russian Revolution. He was doing so in a climate characterized by the enthusiastic attempt to bring about a concrete transfer of anti-bourgeois "Productivist" results into civil society, before a dismal decline that was to last into the postwar years. On the eve of the twenties, his forays into the sector of the applied arts were occasional but, at the same time, already marked by a precise and recognizable visual taste.

In the introduction to the catalogue of the exhibition "5 × 5 = 25," held in Moscow in 1921, Rodchenko declared, along with Alexander Vesnin, Alexandra Exter, Lyubov Popova and Varvara Stepanova, that "Art is finished! It has no place in the human labor apparatus. Labor, technology, organization..."

In 1921–22 he tackled his first commissions in the fields of the theater, films and graphics. From 1923 onward, visual communication became an important area of research and expression; he produced original types of advertisement with the copy produced by Mayakovsky. The two of them became engaged in a fierce struggle against the resistance and incomprehension of a backward-looking, impervious culture that refused to die.

"I was the only one who devoted himself to advertising," Rodchenko wrote of this period in his memoirs. "The texts were to cause me endless problems. They were long-winded, boring, devoid of interest. I corrected the copy myself but it was not easy to persuade clients to accept cuts and abbreviations. Once for example, I had to work on this text: 'He who does not own Dobrolyot [Russian Volunteer Air Fleet] stock, is not a citizen of the USSR.' It was neither a poem nor a slogan. Happening to see the text, Volodya burst out laughing and started making sarcastic remarks. I got angry and rebuked him, telling him that if all good poets could do was to laugh at bad advertisements, there never would be any good advertising. He thought about it and eventually admitted I was right. That was how our collaboration began. In the year and more that I worked for Dobrolyot, I designed posters and other little things. That was really hard work, there was no time for art: their work was new, and interesting. They appreciated my posters. They got used to having me around. Maybe they didn't remember my name, but all of them knew

left: Alexander Rodchenko (Aleksander Mikhailovich Rodchenko, St. Petersburg 1891, Moscow 1956), 1922; in the photograph by M. Kaufman, Alexander Rodchenko is wearing the *prozodezda*, the overalls he designed with Varvara Stepanova in 1922.
below: Alexander Rodchenko's mark/monogram, also visible at bottom right in the poster reproduced on p. 79.

me. I didn't talk about art with them, I didn't propagandize. I worked and that's all. Everything turned out for the best. The Pan-Russian Exhibition was opened. Dobrolyot had organized propaganda-publicity flights of about twenty minutes. The engineer Lazarevich called me in. A would-be intellectual in a pince-nez and a jacket with gold buttons, he said: 'Comrade painter, do me a Futurist poster about the flights.' I was genuinely astonished. And he went on: 'How shall I put it? Something extravagant but not too way out.' I couldn't understand what he was driving at and asked him what he thought of my posters. And I pointed to the ones hanging on the wall. And he: 'They're realistic, yours.' Then I understood and told him: 'No comrade, I have no idea how to do Futurist posters. And the order *à la futuriste* was passed on to a right-wing painter. Later on Comrade Lazarevich found out the secret, or rather a secretary told him. I had made an enemy... " (From Rodchenko's "Notebook" published in issue 6, 1927, of *Novyi Lef*, the magazine for which he had done all the graphics, starting with the covers, since 1923.)

And on the subject of his direct collaborator, Rodchenko continued in his memoirs: "Our trademark was: 'Advertising-Constructors Mayakovsky-Rodchenko.' We worked with great enthusiasm. It was the first real Soviet advertising: it rebelled against the banality of the copy, the little flowers and the other manifestations of petty bourgeois taste so much in vogue in the period of the NEP."

Over the next few years, the "advertising-constructors" produced around fifty memorable posters and a hundred or so signs, wrappers and advertisements for newspapers, pamphlets and projection in cinemas, with aggressive contrasts of flat colors and block-capital lettering. They worked for—among others—GUM (the state department store in Moscow) and the Mospoligraf (Moscow printing house), the Mossel'prom (state grocery concern) and the Rezinotrest (state rubber trust), the publishing houses Molodaya Gvardiya, Gosizdat, Transpecat' and Krasnaya Nov' and the labor unions. "Later on, the work was interrupted," Rodchenko's memoirs conclude mournfully; "... of course the members of the RAPP [Russian Association of Proletarian Writers] and MAPP [Moscow Association of Proletarian Writers] did what they could to harm us, using every means possible and imaginable to discredit us and close down our work. And they won in the end. Naturally, they had very good reason to be worried: the whole of Moscow, all the sales outlets of the Mossel'prom, all the newspapers and magazines were swamped with our adverts... Advertising slowly slid back into the well-worn rut of little texts and little flowers."

76

МАЯКОВСКИЙ УЛЫБАЕТСЯ МАЯКОВСКИЙ СМЕЕТСЯ МАЯКОВСКИЙ ИЗДЕВАЕТСЯ

left: *Mayakovsky Smiles,*
Mayakovsky Laughs,
Mayakovsky Guffaws,
cover of the book, 1923.
Profile of Mayakovsky,
silhouette, 1939.
above: *Books, Leningrad*
Branch of Gosizdat, poster,
1925; the photograph
of Lily Brik, taken
by Alexander Rodchenko,
is from the previous year.
following pages:
two photographs of 1929,
used as back and front cover
of the magazine *Journalist*,
no. 4, 1930.

eric gill stone carver

"Letters are signs for sounds," wrote Eric Gill in the chapter on "Lettering" in *An Essay on Typography*, a true classic in its genre: 1st edition 1931, 2nd expanded edition in 1936, 3rd in 1941, 4th in 1954, 5th in 1988, and they don't stop there. "Letters are not pictures or representations… They are more or less abstract forms… Lettering is for us the Roman alphabet and the Roman alphabet is lettering … and these letters may be said to have reached a permanent type about the 1st century AD… Altho' all sorts of other kinds of lettering existed (on wax tablets, on papyrus, &c.) the most common kind of formal lettering was the inscription in stone. The consequence was that when he made letters 'as well as he could' it was the stone inscription letter that he took as his model. He did not say: Such & such a tool or material naturally makes or lends itself to the making of such and such forms. On the contrary, he said: Letters are such and such forms; therefore, whatever tools & materials we have to use, we must make these forms as well as the tools and material will allow. This order of procedure has always been the one followed. The mind is the arbiter in letter forms, not the tool or the material. This is not to deny that tools and materials have had a very great influence on letter forms. But that influence has been secondary, and for the most part it has been exerted without the craftsman's conscious intention."

Whether you agree or not with these arguments, Gill was one of the most extraordinary artists and visual designers of the 20th century, almost unknown outside his own country. He could be seen as a mature expression of the distinctive "modernism" of the United Kingdom between the wars, played out under the aegis of a restless, flamboyant and inconstant existence, torn between piety and sensuality, asceticism and politics, meditation and propaganda, the sacred and the profane.

Like his personal life (which he recorded in meticulous detail), his artistic and literary output was, to say the least, extravagant and varied: thousands of engravings, over seven hundred inscriptions, at least five hundred sculptures, more than five hundred and fifty texts. And here we must not forget his typefaces, designed between the late twenties and the second half of the thirties but still in use today: Perpetua, Gill Sans, Joanna (the finest italic of the 20th century) the best known, and then Solus, Golden Cockerel and Bunyan (Pilgrim).

An indefatigable orator, fierce polemicist and eloquent writer on art, society and religion, Eric Arthur Rowton Gill was born in Brighton on February 22, 1882, second of the twelve children of Arthur Tidman Gill and Rose Gill. The family had a tradition of religious vocation, starting with his grandfather, a missionary in the South Seas, and continuing with his father, a dissenting minister. The young Eric showed a talent for drawing and in 1897 went to study art at Chichester Technical and Art School.

left: Eric Gill (Brighton 1882, Uxbridge 1940) photographed in his studio at Capel-y-Ffin. below: *The Eye and the Hand*, engraving, 1908; Eric Gill would return several times to this image, used as a personal mark.

this page: text set in 9/11.5 pt.
Monotype Gill Sans.
right: pages reproduced from
An Essay on Typography, 1931.

In 1900, at the age of eighteen, he started work as a draftsman in the London studio of the architect to the Ecclesiastical Commissioners of Westminster, William D. Caröe. During the three years of his apprenticeship with Caröe, Gill spent his evenings studying masonry at Westminster Technical Institute and lettering at the Central School of Art and Design under Edward Johnston. In 1902 Johnston invited him to share his rooms at Lincoln's Inn, one of the four Inns of Court in London. In 1903, Gill decided to leave Caröe's studio and work independently as a letter cutter, after receiving a commission for several inscriptions for the new Medical School in Cambridge from the architect building it, Edward Prior. Johnston married in 1904, and the same year Gill followed his example, marrying Ethel Moore, who was to bear him three daughters (Elizabeth, Petra and Joanna; their son Gordian was adopted). At the outset, Gill worked chiefly on inscriptions, signs and engravings, ordered from him by private individuals as well as the British stationery chain WH Smith and Insel Verlag of Leipzig. After opening his first studio in Hammersmith, he moved with his family to Ditchling, Sussex, where he began to carve stone. Over the course of the years, he was to receive important commissions, such as the stations of the cross for Westminster Cathedral (1914–18) and the reliefs for the London Underground Headquarters (from 1929), BBC Broadcasting House (from 1928) and the council hall of the Palace of Nations in Geneva (1935–38). In 1908, Gill made friends with Roger Fry, Jacob Epstein and Ananda Coomaraswamy, who made a deep and lasting impression on him. Other important meetings took place with Jacques Maritain (1923) and Henry Moore (1928). The community at Ditchling was enriched by the arrival of Johnston in 1912. A year later Gill converted to Catholicism. In 1924, an ever larger community moved from Ditchling to Capel-y-Ffin, a remote, half-ruined monastery in the Welsh Black Mountains, where Gill devoted himself chiefly to engraving and the design of typefaces, in fruitful association with the Monotype Corporation (under the artistic guidance of such an exceptional adviser as Stanley Morison) and the Golden Cockerel Press. In 1924 he received a commission from the government to design postage stamps and a silver coin. The problems posed by the remoteness of Capel-y-Ffin induced him to move again, this time to Piggotts, a group of farms near High Wycombe in the Chilterns. Here, along with various assistants and their families, he set up a sculpture studio and printing works, making the place "a cell of good living in the chaos of our world," as he described it. Finally, in 1939, he designed his only work of architecture (the profession for which he had been trained in his youth), the Neo-Gothic church of Gorleston-on-Sea, near Great Yarmouth. Gill died of lung cancer on November 17, 1940. His tombstone, which he designed himself, is inscribed with the words: "Pray for Me / Eric Gill / Stone Carver."

few extraordinary rational minds can distinguish between a good one & a bad one, or can demonstrate precisely what constitutes A-ness. When is an A not an A? Or when is an R not an R (fig. 17)? It is clear that for any letter there is some sort of norm. To discover this norm is obviously the first thing to be done.

ABCDEFGHIJKLM
NOPQRSTUVWX
Y&Z 1234567890
abcdefghijklmno
pqrstuvwxyz

Figure 15: Monotype sans-serif

¶ The first notable attempt to work out the norm for plain letters was made by Mr Edward Johnston when he designed the sans-serif letter for the London Underground Railways. Some of these letters are not entirely satisfactory, especially when it is remembered that, for such a purpose, an alphabet should be as near as possible 'fool-proof', i.e. the forms should be measurable, patient of dialectical

exposition, as the philosophers would say — nothing should be left to the imagination of the signwriter or the enamel plate maker. In this quality of 'fool-proofness' the Monotype sans-serif face (figure 15) is perhaps an improvement. The letters are more strictly normal — freer from forms depending upon appreciation and critical ability in the workman who has to reproduce them.

¶ But, as there is a norm of letter form — the bare body so to say, of letters — there is also a norm of letter clothes; or rather there are many norms according as letters are used for this place or purpose or that. Between the occasion wherein the pure sans-serif or mono-line (block) letter is appropriate & that in which nothing is more appropriate than pure fancifulness (see fig. 17, 9, 13, 15 & 16), there are innumerable occasions.

¶ A typically moral and conscientious Englishman finds it exceedingly difficult to keep morals out of art talk; he finds himself inclined to think, e.g. that R ought to have a bow more or less semi-circular and of a diameter about half the height of the stem, & a strongly outstanding tail; that an R with a very large bow and hardly any tail at all is wrong. But such moral notions as the word 'ought' implies, &

to make the best jokes about it but even to break the rules with greater assurance (just as a man who knows his road can occasionally jump off it, whereas a man who does not know his road can only be on it by accident), so a good clear training in the making of normal letters will enable a man to indulge more efficiently in fancy and impudence.

(Figure 17 : 1, normal sans-serif; 2–5, unseemly abnormalities & exaggerations; 6, normal with serifs; 7, normal bold; 8, overbold and fatuous; 9–13, 15 and 16, seemly 'fancy' varieties of the normal; 14 & 17, R's with normal bows but tails badly attached.)

¶ But under an industrial system, such as we have in England to-day, the majority of workmen are deprived, not by cruel masters, but by the necessary conditions of machine production, of the ability to exercise any fancy or impudence at all, & are even deprived of any appetite so to do. Fancifulness is therefore within the competence of a smaller and smaller number of workmen. We shall shortly have a situation wherein all jokes and eccentricities are the work of 'designers' — and machine-made jokes reproduced by the million tend to be boring. ¶ The kind of figure 2 shown in fig. 19, or the r's in fig. 20, with violently contrasted thick & thin forms & enor-

Figure 17

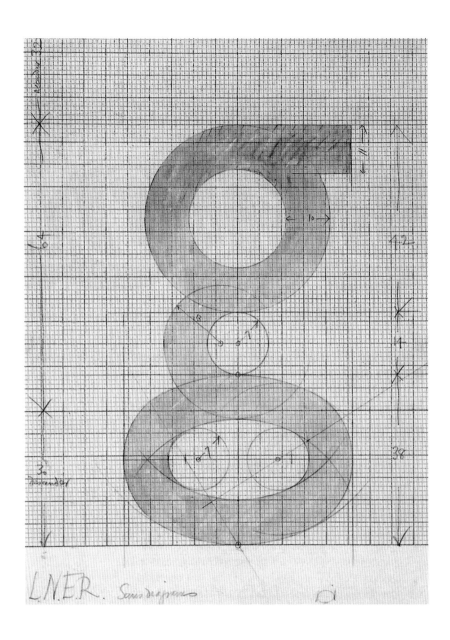

Reproduction of the original
design of the letter "g" of *LNER*,
1928, a typeface devised
for the London & North Eastern
Railway and used for schedules,
signs and announcements; this
typeface would evolve into *Gill
Sans*, brought into production
between 1928 and 1932.

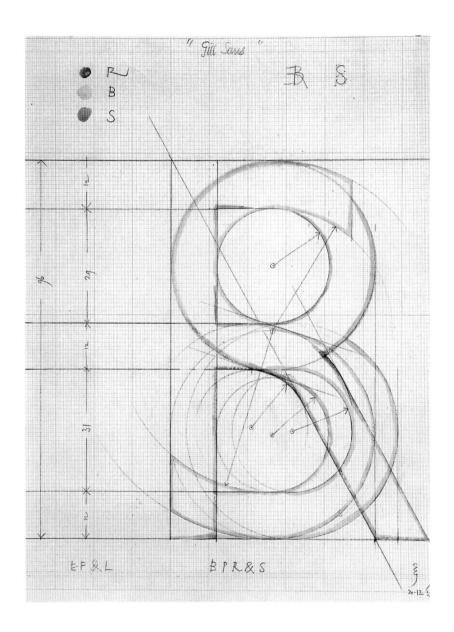

Reproduction of the original
design with study of the letters
"B P R S" and their dimensional
relationships, 1932; the curve
that connects the stem
of the "R" is characteristic
of the alphabets designed by
Eric Gill.

above: *Linear Alphabets*,
engraving, 1931, plate
from *An Essay on Typography*;
right: *Ex-libris: Ananda
Coomaraswamy*, engraving,
1920; Ananda Coomaraswamy
(1877–1947), who touched
on the most diverse themes
of Western and Eastern
thought, rituals, symbolism
and art in over a thousand
publications, was a personal
friend of Eric Gill.
right: *Tobias and Sara*,
bas-relief, 1926, a clear
example of the sensuality
implicit in Eric Gill's work.

jan tschichold faith and reality

In October 1925, the journal *Typographische Mitteilungen* of Leipzig published "Elementary Typography," a landmark in the history of 20th-century graphics that immediately stirred controversy in Germany as well as gathering supporters and making converts. It was soon to become universally famous. It set out its points as follows:

"1 The new typography has an objective purpose. 2 The purpose of typography in general is communication. Communication is achieved in the most succinct, simple and accurate way possible. 3 To fulfill the social functions of typography its components, both internal (contents) and external (consistent use of materials and printing methods), have to be organized. 4 Internal organization signifies limiting ourselves to the basic elements of typography: letters, numerals, symbols, lines of characters...The basic elements of the new typography also include ... the objective image: photography. The basic form of the typeface is sans serif."

The author of this "manifesto"—and designer of the publication—was Jan Tschichold: a twenty-three-year-old calligrapher destined to become one of the greatest visual designers of the 20th century. In August 1923 he found himself on the road to Damascus: visiting the first Bauhaus exhibition in Weimar, he saw the work of teachers at the school and had first-hand experience of the ideas being worked on by the most radical exponents of the avant-garde, such as El Lissitzky, Schwitters and van Doesburg. The effects on his work were immediate.

Of Slavic origin, whence his awkward surname (a transliteration of "people of the Sorbenland"), Tschichold was born in Leipzig on April 2, 1902. From an artistic family—his father Franz was a sign painter—and an aspiring artist himself, he entered the Leipzig Academy in 1919. In 1921, having become an assistant to his professor at the academy, he also began working professionally. Down to the later twenties he designed hundreds of advertisements calligraphically, as was the practice at the time.

At the end of 1925, he set off for Berlin to seek his fortune, found himself a wife in Edith Kramer and worked in Munich. In June 1926 he moved to that city to teach under Paul Renner (then engaged in the design of the epoch-making font Futura). Between the late twenties and early thirties Tschichold also worked on graphics and designed lettering, from an experimental monotype inspired by Albers and called Transit to the dozens of (lost) typefaces for the brand new and not very successful Uhertype machine, the first phototypesetter in history. Above all, he began to write a series of important books (he published more than twenty-five in the course of his life) and designed their layouts. The first of these was a fundamental and famous work published in 1928 (although, for over half a century, accessible only to readers of German) entitled *Die neue Typographie*: the earliest attempt (according to historians) at a theory of the visual design of printed matter.

left: Jan Tschichold
(Leipzig 1902, Locarno 1974) photographed
by Frank Bollinger, 1962.
below: personal logotype, 1925.

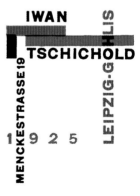

Amidst ideological fireworks, ingenuous declarations of intransigence and frenzies of innovation, Tschichold presented his case for the "new" graphics. It was to be distinguished by functional asymmetry and a machine-oriented rejection of decoration, abstract purity and rhythmic simplicity.

A prominent exponent of Kultur-Bolschewismus (according to the Nazis, who were now in power), he was arrested in the spring of 1933 and, while held in "protective custody" for six weeks, learned he had lost his teaching post. In August 1933 he fled with his wife and four-year-old son to Basel. Given a temporary work permit, he lived in continual difficulties and anxiety until he was granted Swiss citizenship in 1942. From the middle of the thirties, moreover, events led him to regard the categorical assertions of his youth in a different light and to adopt a less obdurate approach to the requirements of visual design, as well as to accept a more reasonable coexistence of tradition and innovation. To many this looked like a betrayal, but his impassioned *auto da fé* contained in *Glaube und Wirklichkeit*, published in June 1946 in response to a violent attack from Max Bill, Tschichold compared the "new typography" to a Teutonic, militarist and absolute desire for regimentation: "The tragedy was that the sincere, ascetic simplicity [of the new typography] soon reached a point beyond which it was impossible to go [and] the search began for new forms, which naturally tended to the other extreme,

Sabon roman
Sabon italic
Sabon bold
Sabon bold italic

decoration... It would be a mistake to consider decorative typography the modern form: both are modern, if we were only to stop investing the word 'modern' with a value judgment." After working for Swiss publishers like Benno Schwabe and Birkhäuser, he went to London immediately after the war, where Allen Lane had the brilliant idea of inviting him to revamp the Penguin editions. From 1947 to 1949, Tschichold took on the immense task of designing books for a mass market, in which the first edition of a normal title ran to not less than 50,000 copies. He established the masterly "Penguin Composition Rules," redesigned the covers and symbols and defined the grids of about twenty series, but categorically refused to fix the typefaces once and for all. He also designed over five hundred title pages, devoting personal attention to each one. Returning to Basel, he continued his activity as a book designer and from 1955 to 1967 was typographic adviser to Hoffmann-La Roche. In the first half of the sixties he designed his best-known font, a "problem-solving" variation of Garamond that was given the name Sabon. In 1968 he retired to Berzona, in Ticino. He left this world on August 11, 1974. "In general, we should consider the typography of the Western world as one and the same thing..." he had declared in New York in 1959, summing up his thinking. "The aim of typography must not be expression, least of all self-expression, but perfect communication achieved by skill. Taking over working principles from previous times or other typographers is not wrong but sensible."

NAPOLEON

PHOEBUS
PALAST

ANFANGSZEITEN:
| 4^{00} | 6^{15} | 8^{30} |

SONNTAGS:
| 1^{45} | 4^{00} | 6^{15} | 8^{30} |

DRUCK: F. BRUCKMANN A.G. MÜNCHEN

sind sie weniger gut als die alten Grotesken. Einen wesentlichen Schritt
nach vorwärts bedeutet die Futura von Paul Renner.
Aber alle bisherigen Bemühungen, die Schrift der neuen Zeit zu schaffen,
gehen nur um eine „Verbesserung" der bisherigen Grotesk; es fehlt allen
diesen Versuchen, die noch viel zu artistisch, zu „künstlerisch" im früheren
Sinne sind, die notwendige grundsätzliche Einstellung.
Ich persönlich glaube, daß es nicht einem einzelnen vorbehalten sein kann,
die Schrift unseres Zeitalters zu schaffen, die von jeder persönlichen Linienführung frei sein müßte. Sie wird das Werk mehrerer sein, unter denen sich
wohl auch ein Ingenieur befinden müßte.
Vorläufig scheinen mir unter allen vorhandenen Groteskschriften die Ak-
zidenzgrotesken (zum Beispiel von Bauer & Co., Stuttgart) wegen ihrer
verhältnismäßig sehr sachlichen und ruhigen Linienführung am geeignetsten.
Schon weniger gut sind die Venus-Grotesk wegen der Versal-E und -F und des gemeinen t (häßliche schräge
Abschnitte der Schäfte). In dritter Linie folgen — wenn nichts Besseres zur
Hand ist — die „malerischen" Blockschriften (magere und fette „Block" usw.)
mit ihren scheinbar angefressenen Rändern und runden Ecken. Die exakten,
konstruktiven Formen der fetten Antiqua, der Aldine und der (alten) Egyptienne
genießen, soweit Auszeichnungsschriften in Betracht kommen, den Vorrang
vor den übrigen Antiquaschriften.
Die grundsätzliche Beschränkung auf diese wenigen Schriftarten bedeutet
indessen nicht, daß Drucker, die über keine oder zu wenig Groteskschrift
verfügen, nicht auch mit anderen Schriftarten zeitgemäße Typographien
gestalten könnten. Aber es muß unbedingt daran festgehalten werden, daß
die Grotesk stets den Vorrang hat und stets besser ist. Ich bin mir wohl
bewußt, daß die Ausschließlichkeit dieser Forderung einen Angriff auf die
romantische Vorliebe nicht geringer Teile der Buchdruckerschaft und des
Publikums für die alten verzierten Buchstabenformen darstellt. Diese alten
Schriften können übrigens zuweilen in der modernen Typographie eine neue
Anwendung finden: als Witz, wo es sich zum Beispiel darum handelt, die
„gute alte Zeit" typographisch zu parodieren; als Blickfang unter Groteskschriften (zum Beispiel ein großes Fraktur-B) usw. (wie etwa die pompösen
wilhelminischen Generals- und Admiralsfräcke zu Portieruniformen und
Maskenballanzügen degradiert worden sind). Wer so an der Fraktur, dieser
Kanzlistenschrift des 16. Jahrhunderts, hängt, daß er nicht von ihr lassen
kann, sollte sie dann doch nicht durch eine unserer Zeit gemäße Grup-
pierung, die nie zu ihr passen kann, vergewaltigen. Die Fraktur, ebenso
wie Gotisch und Schwabacher, hat so wenig mit uns zu tun, daß sie als
Aufbauform zeitgemäßer Typographie vollkommen ausschaltet.

76

Der betont nationale, partikularistische Charakter der Fraktur, aber auch
der entsprechenden Nationalschriften anderer Völker, zum Beispiel des
Russischen oder Chinesischen, widerspricht den heutigen übernationalen
Bindungen der Völker und zwingt zu ihrer unabwendbaren Beseitigung.[*]
An ihr festzuhalten, ist Rückschritt. Die lateinische Schrift ist die internationale Schrift der Zukunft. Allerdings bedarf diese noch ganz beträcht-
licher Veränderungen, wenn sie den wirtschaftlichen Bedingungen der
Neuzeit entsprechen und den technischen Formen der Gegenwart und gar
der Zukunft ebenbürtig sein will.
Ebensowenig wie die Fraktur kommen jene Lateinschriften in Frage, die durch
ihre besondere Form fesseln (z.B. Schreib- und Zierschriften, Eckmann u.ä.).
Die Einzelheiten solcher Buchstaben lenken das Interesse vom Inhalt ab
und widersprechen so dem Wesen der Typographie, die nie Selbstzweck ist.
Ihre parodierende Anwendung, in dem schon oben bezeichneten Sinne,
bleibt natürlich offen.
Als Brotschrift ist die heutige Grotesk nur bedingt geeignet. Ein fetter
Schnitt kommt kaum in Frage, da sich fette Grotesk im fortlaufenden Satz
zu schwer liest. Die besten Erfahrungen machte ich mit der sogenannten
Gewöhnlichen Akzidenzgrotesk, die ein ruhiges und bequem lesbares Bild
ergibt. Indem ich dieses Buch aus einer solchen Grotesk setzen ließ, wollte
ich nachweisen, daß man sie sehr gut lesen kann; im übrigen habe ich an
ihr noch mancherlei auszusetzen. Trotzdem aber zog ich sie allen Antiqua-

* In Rußland, der Türkei und China sind von Staats wegen Bestrebungen im Gange, die dort noch allein-
gültigen Nationalschriften durch Gesetz abzuschaffen und sie durch die lateinische Schrift zu ersetzen. In
Deutschland dagegen werden die lateinischen Aufschriften der Bahnhöfe durch solche in gotischer (für den
Ausländer fast unleserlicher) Schrift ersetzt. Auch ein „Fortschritt"!

77

JOHANNES MOLZAHN:
Typosignet für die Eisenwarenfabrik
Wilhelm Heunert, Soest

größerer Formen und die starke Kraft, die allen Dingen innewohnt, deren
Äußeres ganz aus einem technischen Herstellungsprozeß hervorgeht.
Die Mittel, die dem Buchdrucker bei der Gestaltung von Signeten zur Ver-
fügung stehen, sind die typographischen Formen des Setzkastens: Linien,
Bogen, die geometrischen Formen, Buchstaben, und — nicht zuletzt — die
Phantasie. Ohne sie nützen einem selbst die neuesten Messingstücke und
Schriften nichts
Das Signet bringt meist Buchstaben in neuartiger Form, ein Symbol der
Ware oder beides zugleich. Die Wirkung des Signets für Pelikan beruht auf
der Verwendung einfachster Typoformen von kontrastierenden Stärken und
Bewegungen. Das Signet „Heunert" ist ein Sinnbild für die Eisenwaren der
Firma, zusammengesetzt aus dem Initial des Namens Heunert. Mit dem Initial

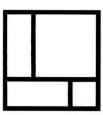

HERBERT BAYER:
Typosignet für einen Glasmaler

114

des Vornamens Piet zusammen wird das schwarze Quadrat („zwart" ist die
holländische Form des deutschen „schwarz") zu einer unvergeßlichen Marke.
Ähnlich dem Heunertsignet gibt das Typosignet für einen Glasmaler von
Herbert Bayer ein zusammengedrängtes Sinnbild des Berufs: die Abstraktion
der Linien eines Glasfensters.
Wenngleich es sehr zu begrüßen wäre, wenn sich der Buchdrucker mehr
als bisher auch der Gestaltung von Signeten zuwenden würde, muß aber auf
das eindringlichste davor gewarnt werden, mit dem Setzkasten hergestellte
bloße Buchstabenverbindungen (Monogramme) als Signete anzusehen, sie
zu schaffen und sie gar zu verwenden. Ein Signet ist etwas durchaus anderes.
Höheres als das bloße Monogramm, und ein mangelhaftes Signet viel schlim-
mer als gar keines. Der Buchdrucker ist heute oft verführt, an die Stelle des
früheren Schmuckstücks ein Typomonogramm zu setzen. Aber nur das Signet
ist auf Werbsachen berechtigt; Monogramme haben dort in unserer Zeit
keinen Sinn. Ein Monogramm als Warenmarke ist stets schlechter als ein
Signet. Und ein schlechtes Signet kann zum Grundfehler einer Werbung
werden. Darum verzichte man lieber auf das Monogramm als Signetersatz,
wenn zu einem Typosignet die Zeit, die man dazu unbedingt braucht, fehlt,
und beschränke sich auf die bloße Schrift.
Jedenfalls aber bietet das Typosignet dem Buchdrucker die Möglichkeit einer
anregenden und dankbaren Betätigung, und die Schwierigkeiten eines guten
Signets sollten nur ein Ansporn zu ihrer Bewältigung sein.

PIET ZWART: Eigenmarke (Typosignet)

8*

115

left: pages reproduced from
The New Typography, 1928.
above: *Philobiblon*, poster
in gold and black for
a bookstore in Warsaw, 1924.

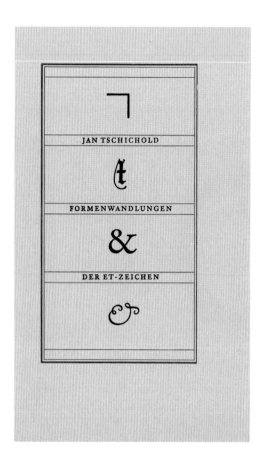

JAN TSCHICHOLD

FORMENWANDLUNGEN

&

DER ET-ZEICHEN

left: *The Formal Evolution of the Ampersand*, cover of the book written by Jan Tschichold, 1950; the text and illustrations examine the typographical changes in the conjunction "et," commonly known as the "e commerciale" in Italian and the ampersand in English.
below: *The Flight from Time*, cover of the book by the Dadaist Hugo Ball from Zurich, 1944.
right: *The Sonnets, and A Lover's Complaint*, back and front cover of an edition of William Shakespeare, 1947; prototype of a successful series, it is perhaps Jan Tschichold's best-known work for Penguin Books.

HUGO BALL

DIE FLUCHT AUS DER ZEIT

THE PENGUIN SHAKESPEARE

The following volumes have so far been issued: several are at present out of print, but new editions are in preparation. Further volumes will follow in due course.

ANTONY AND CLEOPATRA
AS YOU LIKE IT
CORIOLANUS
HAMLET
HENRY IV, PART I
HENRY IV, PART II
HENRY V
JULIUS CAESAR
KING LEAR
MACBETH
THE MERCHANT OF VENICE
A MIDSUMMER NIGHT'S DREAM
MUCH ADO ABOUT NOTHING
OTHELLO
RICHARD II
ROMEO AND JULIET
THE SONNETS
THE TEMPEST
TROYLUS AND CRESSIDA
TWELFTH NIGHT
A WINTER'S TALE

One shilling and sixpence each

PENGUIN BOOKS

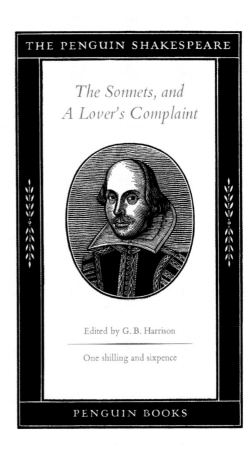

THE PENGUIN SHAKESPEARE

*The Sonnets, and
A Lover's Complaint*

Edited by G. B. Harrison

One shilling and sixpence

PENGUIN BOOKS

ZURICHTUNG
SIEHE HIER
↓

nicht
größer!   ALTERNATIVE

ZURICHTUNG SO

BITTE DIESE 8 BUCHSTABEN NICHT ALS MODELLE BENUTZEN

Neue Zeichnungen für die SABON von Jan Tschichold für die Grade von 14 Punkt ab. Mai 1965

Fertig 20/5/65
— 18 XI 65

2. Mai 1965

Der Neuschnitt vom 11.8.65
stimmt nicht mit
dieser Zeichnung. Ist oben
zu breit, und nach
links gedreht.
Endstrich oben rechts
ist ganz anders als
in der Vorlage.
Die Hauptbewegung
ist hier gelähmt.

fl ist in der
Mitte zu
verbinden.
Sonst müßte
man ja auch
fi in der Mitte
trennen!

ft ist unbedingt nötig,
weil wir sonst zu wenig
obere Bogen haben.
Bitte analog dem
fl in der Stärke
korrigieren.

← hier ist das
normale c. Der Tropfen war
anders. Bitte ck entsprechend
korrigieren

↑ bleibt
unverändert.

Korrigiert   Korrigiert   Korrigiert

27.8.65 Tschichold

98

faffüßïft?

umühlins

Unt

a b c d ε E f g h ij k l m
N O p q r s T U V W X y z

left and above: reproductions
of the original designs of the *Sabon*
typeface, 1965; Jan Tschichold
started work on it in 1960,
with the aim of bringing
onto the market a font similar
to *Garamond*, utilizable both
for hand composition and for
linotyping and phototypesetting.
Brought into production in 1967,
Sabon owes its name to Jacques
(Jakob) Sabon, a French
typographer who introduced the
punches of Claude Garamond
(1480–1561) to Frankfurt in the
middle of the 16th century.
above: *Universal* typeface, 1928;
an early work, it reflects an opposite
direction in research to that
of *Sabon*; compare with p. 114.

kurt schwitters merz ist form: the art of typography

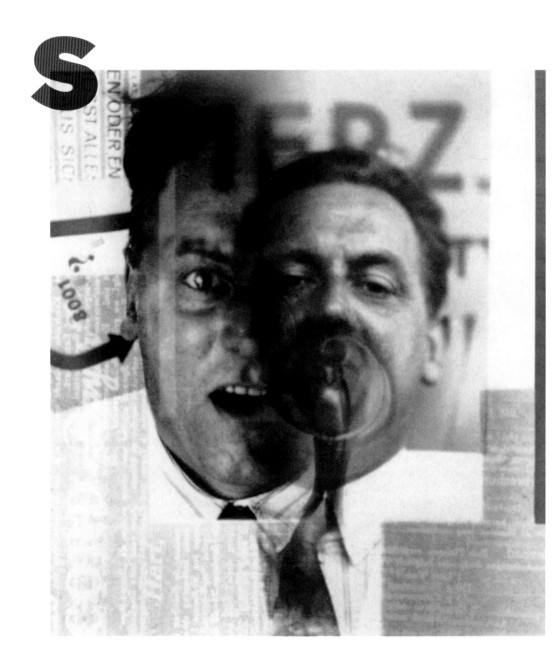

A powerful wave of (aesthetic) remodeling of the universe swept through the artistic avant-garde in the early 20th century, especially between the end of the second decade and the early thirties. It affected the entire range of movements and groups, some quite long-lived, and influenced proclamations and manifestos of every sort.

This tempestuous swirl of ideas, which from the time of the early futurist movements had continued to reverberate through the most significant research carried out by highly active squads of artists in Europe and beyond, did not spare the field of graphics. In fact it was the object of close, continuous attention, though it rather petered out in the second half of the century.

However contradictory it may appear in the tumultuous dialectic between order and disorder so typical of the "historical avant-garde," it was one of the most radical of the Dadaists who devoted the most sustained thought to graphics as a means of communication and crux of design. This was Kurt Schwitters, inventor of a distinctive form of plastic and pictorial expression founded on the exploitation of junk and chance, of the residual and fragmentary taken from daily life and elevated to the status of true artifacts. Throughout his life he worked to develop an ironic philosophy of art, summing it up in a formula, "Merz," a label that he applied to all his work, from his continuous pictorial experiments to his few but highly significant environmental projects (which he called *Merzbau*) and even his work as a graphic artist and letter designer.

Kurt Hermann Eduard Karl Julius Schwitters was born in 1887 in Hanover, the city where he commenced his higher education at the Kunstgewerbeschule (1908–09), completing his studies at the Kunstakademie in Dresden (1909–14). After the tragic disruption of the Great War, his first exhibition at the Der Sturm gallery in Berlin (1918) was followed by two events (1919) of great significance: the first *Merzbilden* and the collection of poems *Anna Blume Dichtungen*. Research in the field of the sound continuum, which led him to embark on bold experiments in concrete poetry and phonetic and verbal composition such as the *Ursonate* (1921), was another important strand in Schwitters' complex body of work. In 1920 he made friends with Jean Arp and Raoul Hausmann, two of the avant-garde artists most in tune with his own ideas. In 1921 he made a trip to Prague with Hannah Höch and Raoul Hausmann, staging demonstrative lectures along the way. After encountering (1922) Theo van Doesburg, an unorthodox and intransigent propagandist for the arts, he organized a Dada-tournée with him in the Netherlands (1923). The experience proved decisive in both men's development.

Soon afterward, Schwitters began his first *Merzbau*, founded the Merzverlag publishing house and started working as a graphic designer with the Werbezentrale advertising agency. In the experimental magazine *Merz* (its issue in 1923 was devoted to Holland Dada) he published some important articles on graphics. They included

left: Kurt Schwitters (Hanover 1887, Ambleside 1948) in a photomontage by El Lissitzky, 1924.
below: *Merz*, logotype, 1923.

El Lissitzky's "Topography of Typography," which appeared in issue no. 4, and his "Theses on Typography," in no. 11 (1924), as well as the monographic *Typoreklame Pelikannummer*, which coincided with Max Burchartz's celebrated manifesto *Gestaltung der Reklame*. (Burchartz was a partner with Johannes Canis in the Werbe-Bau agency in Bochum.)

The outcome of all this application to typographic questions, in the vein of the reform of the alphabet so strong in Germany, was the invention (1972) of the "Neue Plastische Systemschrift" (new plastic writing system). His experiments culminated in the optophonetic "f" version: "systematic writing requires that the complete image of writing matches all the sounds of the language." Schwitters published it in issue 8/9 of the Dutch magazine *10* and used it in numerous posters. His participation (1927) in the "Die Abstrakten Hanover" group was followed by membership of the international "Abstraction-Création" movement (1932), while the foundation of the "Ring neuer Werbegestalter" (1927) saw him at the center of an elite group of activists of the "new typography" (Baumeister, Bayer, Bill, Burchartz, Cassandre, Domela, Heartfield, Kassak, Moholy-Nagy, Stam, Sutnar, Teige, Trump, Tschichold, van Doesburg, Vordemberge-Gildewart and Zwart, among others). He was the driving force in the group and organized its exhibitions (over twenty, in Cologne, Hamburg, Berlin, Stockholm, Basel, Copenhagen, Amsterdam and Rotterdam between 1928 and 1931).

The most convincing expression of Schwitters' ideas to come out of this experience in the field was the booklet *Die neue Gestaltung in der Typographie* (1930). As part of the state policy of Rationalisierung, the municipality of Hanover entrusted him (1929–34) with the task of redesigning its visual identity, a mission that Schwitters undertook methodically. His aim, he declared in *Über die einheitliche Gestaltung von Drucksachen* (1930) was to "understand what is identical, respecting as far as possible its similarities; what is different, respecting as far as possible its characteristics; what is analogous, respecting as far as possible its affinities." The result was an extraordinary example of a coordinated public image. Proposing a distinctive pictogram for the city, Schwitters designed a "logical scheme" for its stationery and forms, as well as the printed material of the transport system, the municipal theater and the opera house, using DIN formats and the Futura type.

After the Nazis took power (1933), Schwitters sought refuge first in Norway (settling at Lysaker, in 1937, where be began another *Merzbau*) and then in Great Britain (where he was initially interned for seventeen months on the Isle of Man).

Moving to Ambleside at the end of the Second World War, he started work on his third *Merzbau* (1947), shortly before his death at the beginning of 1948. So ended a career in which he had exhaustively tested the thesis expounded in *Merz* 11 as far back as 1924: "Typographie kann unter Umständen Kunst sein."

	Prinzip der ORIENTIERUNG	Prinzip der WERBUNG
Briefkopf		
Briefumschlag		
Rechnung		
Vordruck		
Prospekt		
Postkarte		
Plakat		
Broschüre		
Buch		
Inserat		
Programm		
Katalog		
Eintrittskarte		
Packung		
Erlaß		
Lichtreklame		

1

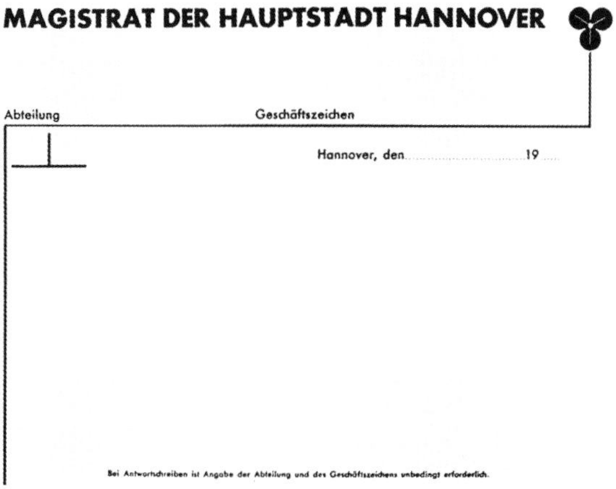

MAGISTRAT DER HAUPTSTADT HANNOVER

Abteilung   Geschäftszeichen

Hannover, den .... 19....

Bei Antwortschreiben ist Angabe der Abteilung und des Geschäftszeichens unbedingt erforderlich.

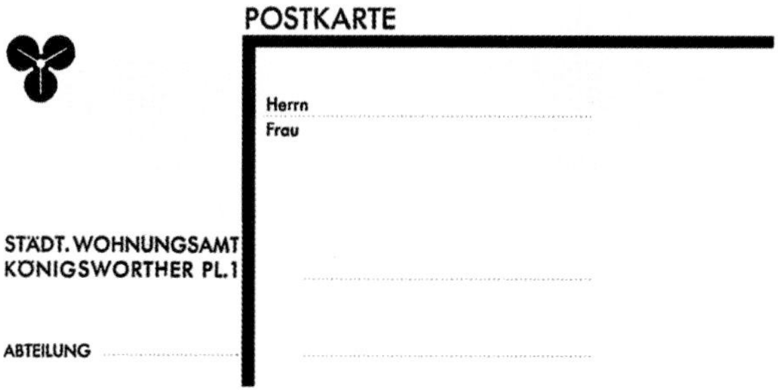

POSTKARTE

Herrn
Frau

STÄDT. WOHNUNGSAMT
KÖNIGSWORTHER PL.1

ABTEILUNG

left: letter paper and postcard, 1930; these are two examples of the hundreds of different kinds of printed matter produced by the municipality of Hanover to the design of Kurt Schwitters, practitioner of both Dadaist agitprop and systematic graphics, with only apparent inconsistency.

above: Kurt Schwitters
declaiming in London,
sequence of photographs
by Ernst Schwitters, 1944.
right: *Systematic Plastic
Typification*, digital reproduction
of the author's name
as it appears in the first study
table, 1927; in this sort of
alphabetical phoneticization,
Kurt Schwitters emphasizes
the sonority of the vowels
by thickening them and varying
their geometry with respect
to the consonants.

KURT SCHWITTERS

KURT SCHWITTERS

KURT SCHWITTERS

KURT SCHWITTERS

MAGISTRAT DER HAUPTSTADT HANNOVER
Magistrat der Stadt
PORTOPFLICHTIGE DIENSTSACHE

left: *Official Document
with Requirement for Stamp,*
collage, 1931–32; "improper"
recycling of the municipality
of Hanover's line of paper.
above: *For Tschichold,*
mixed media, 1927.

Inhalt: DADA IN HOLLAND. KOK: GEDICHT. BONSET: GEDICHT; AAN ANNA BLOEME.

PICABIA: ZEICHNUNG. HANNAH HÖCH: ZEICHNUNG; WEISSLACKIERTE TÜTE

MERZ
1
HOLLAND ■
DADA

JANUAR 1923
HERAUSGEBER: KURT SCHWITTERS
HANNOVER · WALDHAUSENSTRASSE 5ⁱⁱ

DA
DA X DA
DA

above: *Merz*, cover
of the magazine, no. 1, 1923;
dedicated to Dutch Dadaism.
right: *Merzbau*, Hanover 1933.

bauhaus type, typography, typophoto

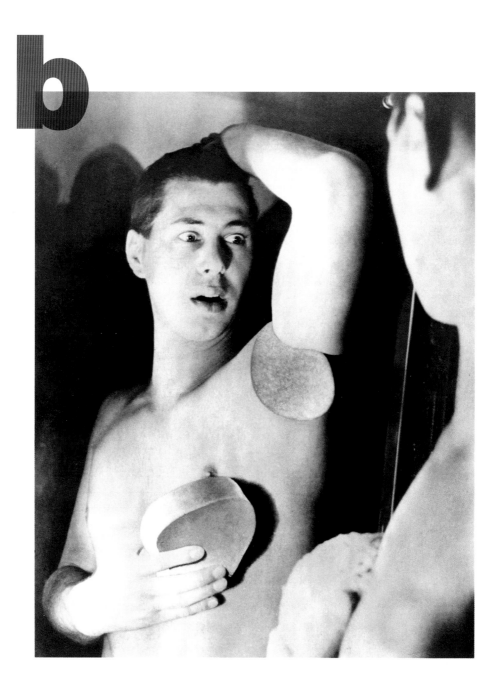

In this at least, the myth lives up to the facts: in the field of graphics, the Bauhaus represents one of the highest peaks attained in the research carried out in the early 20th century, destined to have a lasting influence on subsequent developments. "In the Bauhaus at Weimar," explained Herbert Bayer in 1928, in *Typography and Advertising Graphics*, "an art press was used for the reproduction of graphic works... When the workshops of the new Bauhaus building in Dessau were set up ... a small printing works was installed as a teaching workshop. In the handling of orders, students were able to get practice in setting by hand, makeup and printing. No fashionable aestheticisms, in the sense of 'consumer graphics,' but a work inspired by an awareness of the aims and of the better use of typographic material, up until then held back by an antiquated tradition."

In effect, the teaching and production of the early period of the Bauhaus, the institute founded at Weimar by Walter Gropius in 1919 (with the never fulfilled intention of making it, primarily, a school of architecture) was limited to the realization of art prints (entrusted to the skills of Carl Zaubitzer, under the direction of Lyonel Feininger). The graphic artifacts that interest us (a few posters, postcards and not much else, when all is said and done) are, for the mostpart, characterized by a calligraphic-primitivist stamp, linked to the taste of the teacher of the Vorkurs, the preliminary course, Johannes Itten. It is necessary to wait until the first major exhibition of the Bauhaus, in 1923, to see a renewal in the approach (partly through the efforts of Oskar Schlemmer, commencing with the mark of 1922), vigorously supported by a new teacher, the Hungarian Laszlo Moholy-Nagy.

An outstanding exponent of European avant-garde art, Moholy-Nagy was appointed to a teaching post (he was put in charge of the metalworking department) in April 1923 and immediately made himself an advocate of a radical shift "from the palette to the machine." Not coincidentally, he wrote in 1923, "Typography is an instrument of communication. It must communicate clearly in the most urgent form. Clarity must be emphasized because, in comparison with prehistoric pictographs, it is the essence of script... Therefore, above all, unambiguous clarity in all typography. Legibility of communication must never be allowed to suffer for an aesthetic code adopted in advance." "A typographical construction is modern," he continued in 1926, two years before leaving the Bauhaus and moving to Berlin, "if it derives the means that it adopts from its own internal laws... The element that characterizes the technique of our current work and that is crucial for its development is the exploitation of the possibilities offered by machinery. Our modern typographic products ... will have to have the characteristics of clarity, concision and precision."

So he was responsible for the emergence of a specific interest in typography and for the equipment (mentally and practically) of the Bauhaus for this sector, along prophetic lines that envisaged the transition from a static kind of graphics to a form of dynamic

left: Herbert Bayer (Haag 1900, Santa Barbara 1985) in a photographic self-portrait, 1932. The Austrian Herbert Bayer studied at the Bauhaus between 1921 and 1923; in 1925 he became "young teacher" and was put in charge of the typographic workshop, at Dessau. He emigrated to the US in 1938. below: the imprint designed by Laszlo Moholy-Nagy for the Bauhaus editions, 1923.

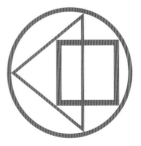

above: Oskar Schlemmer
(Stuttgart 1888, Baden-Baden
1943) in a photograph
by Hugo Ertfurt, 1927.
Oskar Schlemmer taught
at the Bauhaus from 1921
to 1929 in the wall decoration,
sculpture and theater
workshops; he toured
with the "Bauhaus Ballet"
in Germany and Switzerland.
right: *New Art Salon*, poster
for an exhibition of figurative
art by Oskar Schlemmer, 1913;
others would use the theme
of the stylized face
in the communication
of the Bauhaus, in a variety
of ways.

hybridization between text and image, to a visual synopsis borrowed from his passion for experimentation with photography and film. "Form, representation," explained Moholy-Nagy in his first book, *Malerei Photographie Film*, in 1925, "is founded on optical and associative relations: toward a visual, associative, conceptual, synthetic continuity; toward the typophoto as an unambiguous representation, through an optically effective form... What is the typophoto? Typography is communication composed with type. Photography is the visual rendering of what can be captured optically. Typophoto is the visually most exact rendering of communication."

In the field of graphic production, his most important contribution was the innovative conception of the series of *Bauhausbücher*: Moholy-Nagy took personal charge of twelve of the fourteen "Bauhaus books" that were brought out between 1925 (the first eight were ready in 1924) and 1931, even designing some of their covers. Along with him, other teachers—such as Josef Albers, who took over from Moholy-Nagy in the preliminary course, Herbert Bayer and Joost Schmidt—further developed the idea of a "new typography," with regard both to the design of lettering (aiming at the "monoalphabet" envisaged by Portsmann, as in the case of Bayer's Universal of 1926) and to that of graphic communication through printed matter, in a series of extraordinary experiments. Trained first at Linz and Darmstadt, Bayer came to the Bauhaus to complete his studies in 1921 and then was appointed a teacher at the new school in Dessau (after a journey to Italy in 1923–24) and was placed in charge of the printing shop from 1925 to 1928. He then left the Bauhaus and moved to Berlin where (among other things) he worked at the Dorland agency, before emigrating to the US in 1938, on the eve of the war.

Having graduated in painting from the College of Fine Arts in Weimar in 1914, Joost Schmidt studied sculpture at the Bauhaus, and was entrusted with the direction of that workshop in 1925. Following the departure of Bayer, he took over the running of the printing shop (1928–32) until the closure of the school, and also distinguished himself by his work in the field of exhibition design (an area to which his predecessor had devoted considerable attention as well). The compositional principles of typography at the Bauhaus, initially derived from the neoplasticism of van Doesburg and Russian constructivism, had gradually been consolidated over the course of time and through practice, with the introduction of considerations of economics and scientific management, of maximum efficiency and economy of means.

Despite the efforts of the teachers, however, the outcome of this was the spread of the idea of a Bauhaus "style." "The result was the rapid adoption," Bayer summed up bitterly "of banal external appearances ... what was left was the abuse of large dots, thick bars, flourishes and imitations of nature with typographic materials but, in that way, things were right back where they started."

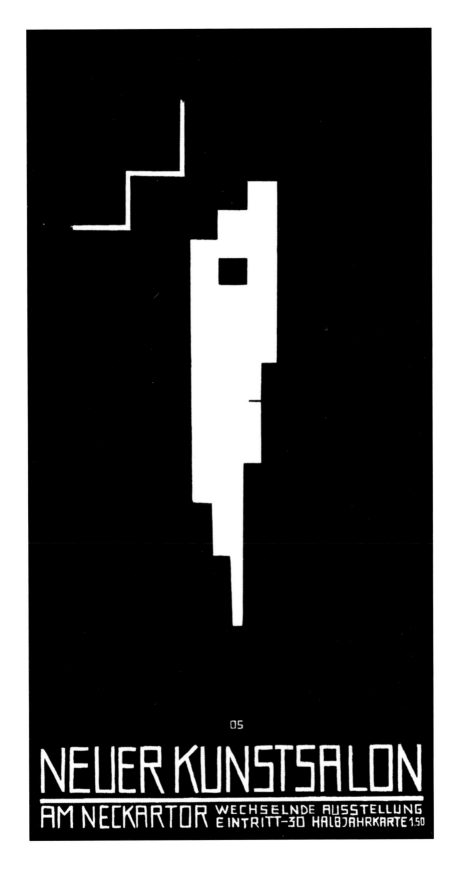

abcdefghi
jklmnopqr
stuvwxyz

HERBERT BAYER: Abb. 1. Alfabet
„g" und „k" sind noch als
unfertig zu betrachten

Beispiel eines Zeichens
in größerem Maßstab
Präzise optische Wirkung

sturm blond

Abb. 2. Anwendung

left: *Universal* typeface,
designed by Herbert Bayer,
presentation plate, 1924–25.
It is exemplary of the
typographical research
carried out at and around
the Bauhaus (p. 99): the
extreme geometricization
of the letters is achieved
at the expense of the harmony
of the composition and
of legibility, and the wholly
ideological economy
of the design induces the author
not to introduce optical
corrections; compare with
p. 126.
right: *The New Line*, magazine
covers by Herbert Bayer,
October 1934, July 1935;
as the masthead demonstrates,
one possible use
of the *Universal* typeface
is as a logotype.

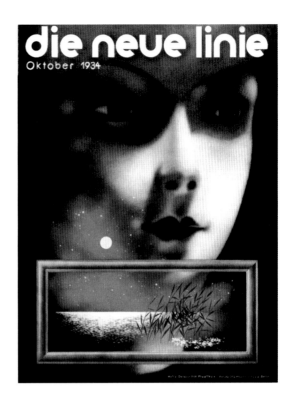

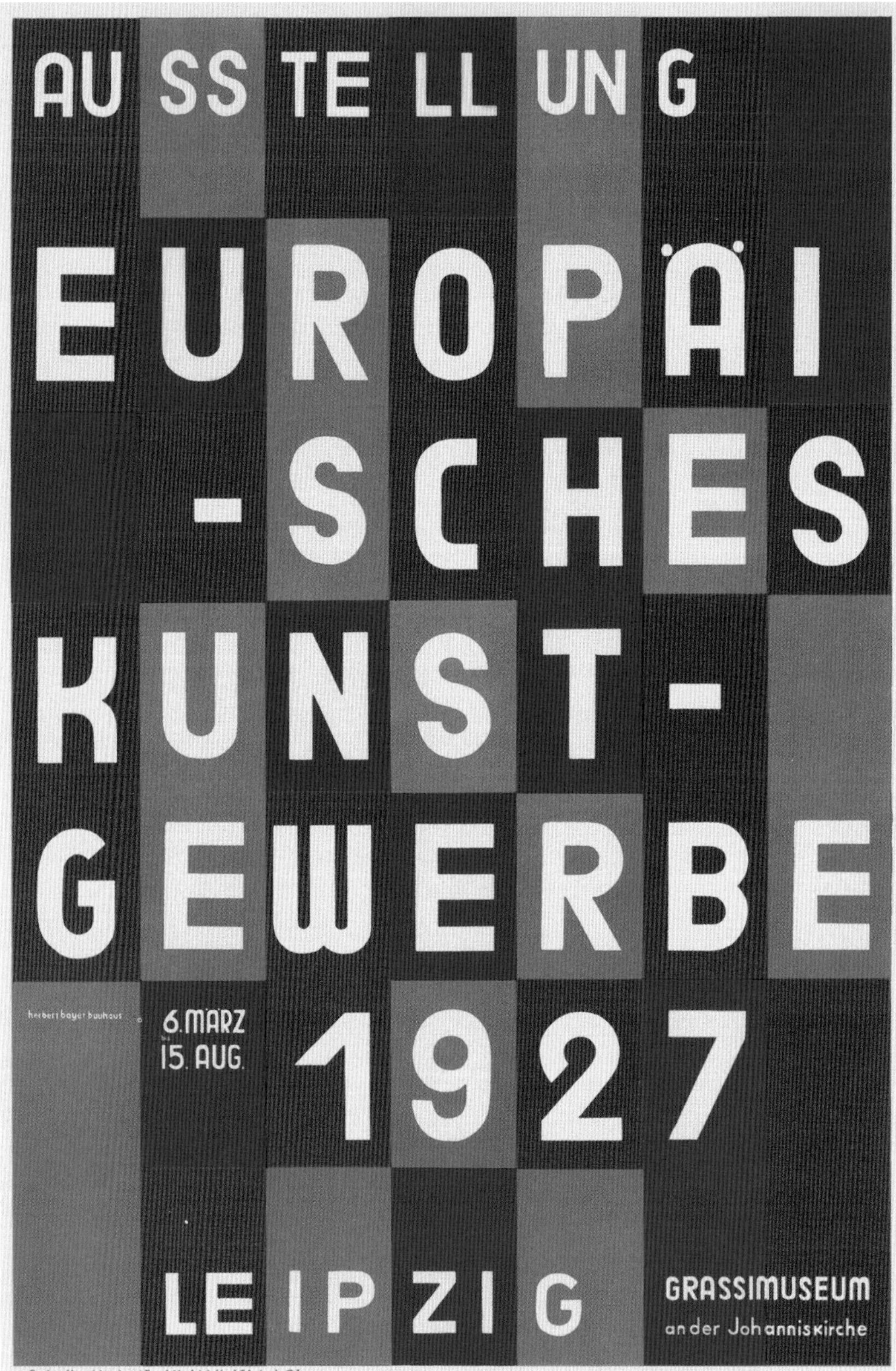
AUSSTELLUNG
EUROPÄI-SCHES KUNST-GEWERBE
herbert bayer bauhaus
6. MÄRZ
15. AUG.
1927
LEIPZIG
GRASSIMUSEUM
an der Johanniskirche
Buch-u Kunstdruckerei Ernst Hedrich Nachf Leipzig C1

left: *Exhibition
of European Applied Art
in Leipzig*, poster
by Herbert Bayer, 1927.
above: *Bauhaus Exhibition
in Basel*, poster
by Franz Ehrlich executed using
typefaces by Joost Schmidt,
1929.
below: Joost Schmidt
(Wurnstorf 1893, Nuremberg
1948) in a photograph from
1930; Joost Schmidt attended
the Bauhaus between 1919
and 1925, and taught there
from 1925 to 1932, directing
the sculpture and advertising
workshops; he made a
considerable contribution
in the field of exhibition design.

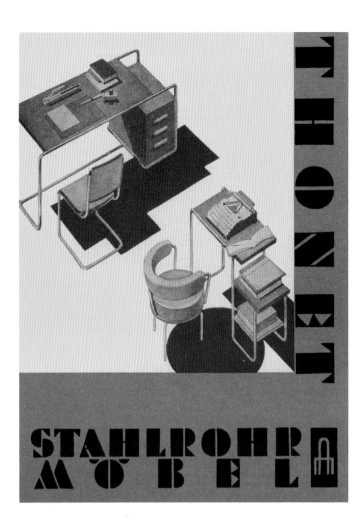

left: *Thonet Tubular Metal Furniture*, cover of advertising brochure by Kurt Schmidt, 1930.
below and below right: *Modular Typeface* by Josef Albers, template in opal glass and reproduction of the presentation plate, 1931. A limited series of geometric shapes (circle, rectangle, half circle, quarter circle, rectangle+quarter circle) are used to compose the lower and uppercase alphabets in a sort of stencil typeface; compare with p. 204.
right: Josef Albers (Bottrop 1888, Orange 1976) seated on the definitive prototype of the Wassily armchair designed by Marcel Breuer in a photograph by Umbo (Otto Umbehr), 1928. Josef Albers was a student at the Bauhaus between 1920 and 1923, and taught there from that year until 1933, when he emigrated to the US; he directed the preparatory course and the joinery workshop.

abcdefghijklmnop
qrfstuvwxyzk123
ABCDEFGHIJKLMNO
PQRSTUVWXYZäéš

above: Laszlo Moholy-Nagy
(Bácsbarsod 1895, Chicago
1946) in a photograph
by Vories Fischer, 1946.
The Hungarian Laszlo Moholy-
Nagy taught at the Bauhaus
from 1923 to 1928, where he
was in charge of the metal
workshop and the preparatory
course; he was responsible
for the school's image and the
advertising of its publications;
in 1937 he founded
the Chicago Bauhaus (School
of Design), directing it up until
his death.
left: *Broom*, photograms for
the cover, no. 4, March 1922.
right: *Building in France,
Building in Iron, Building
in Reinforced Concrete*, cover
of the book by Sigfried Giedion,
1928.

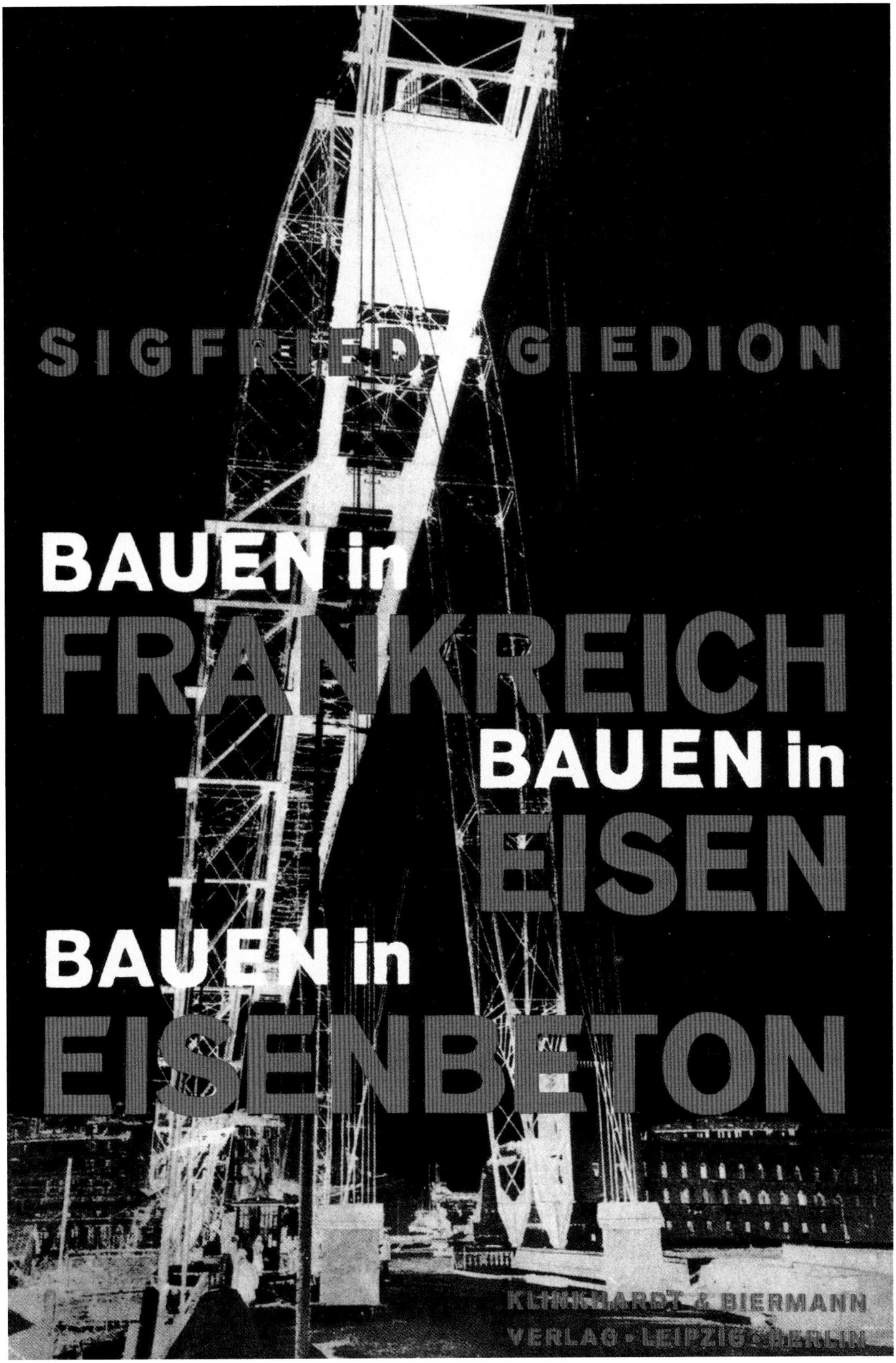

SIGFRIED GIEDION

BAUEN in
FRANKREICH
BAUEN in
EISEN
BAUEN in
EISENBETON

KLINKHARDT & BIERMANN
VERLAG · LEIPZIG · BERLIN

paul renner & paul rand two 20th-century masters

Scholarly literature and specialist books are some people's stock-in-trade, an essential source of knowledge or stimulus to thought. Such people are sure to find it strange, certainly significant and somewhat disconcerting that there should be such a shortage or even complete absence of reliable reference works, accurate standard monographs and specific studies about the life and works of many acclaimed masters, recognized innovators and fundamental figures in the sciences and the arts. Perhaps this is due to the general consensus surrounding the reputations and names of such figures, or perhaps just to a culpable measure of laziness on the part of scholars in the face of undisputed excellence. For instance, in the field of 20th-century graphics and visual design, this was the fate, till quite recently, of Paul Renner, the assiduous German interpreter of the *Zeitgeist* and author of the universally appreciated typeface Futura (1924–28), and also of Paul Rand, an extraordinarily talented American graphic designer and perfect exponent of the equivocal indigenous "modernism," best-known for his IBM trademark (1956).

Paul Renner

The very fine output of the London publisher Hyphen Press, run by Robin Kinross (author of the acute and popular *Modern Typography: An Essay in Critical History*, 1992, 1994) has accustomed us to rare and valuable writings on the history of graphics and typography in the 20th century, such as *Designing Books*, devoted to the work of the Swiss Jost Hochuli. The book by Christopher Burke entitled *Paul Renner: The Art of Typography*, London 1998, is the very first study devoted to this exemplary typographer and designer of German lettering. (It grew out of the author's research for a doctoral thesis at the University of Reading, perhaps the most specialized in the world for typography.) Very scholarly and sparingly but appropriately illustrated (a pity about the heavy-handed cover, not up to the publisher's usual standards), Burke's book examines the entire span of Renner's artistic career and life.

Born in 1878 in Prussia ("Prussian" is how he described himself in a curriculum vitae of 1925) and given a strictly religious upbringing by his father, an evangelical theologian, Renner's work embodies the central themes of German culture in the first half of the 20th century. Trained as an artist at the fine arts academies in Berlin, Karlsruhe and Munich and initially active as a painter in the circle of the "Munich cultural Renaissance" of the early 1900s, he was attracted to book design. He attended a school of applied arts in Munich, where Hermann Obrist also taught. He was one of the first and staunchest members of the Deutscher Werkbund, taking an active part in all of the association's work and fierce debates. He worked for a short while at the Kunstschule in Frankfurt (where he came into contact with Ferdinand Kramer, active in the standardization department under Ernst May) in the mid-twenties, the period when he started work on the Futura typeface. In 1926 he returned to Munich, where he was appointed director of what would come to be known as the Graphische Berufschule,

Futura book
Futura book oblique
Futura heavy
Futura heavy oblique
Futura bold
Futura bold
Futura bold oblique
Futura extra bold
Futura extra bold oblique

a famous school of graphic art whose teachers also included Jan Tschichold (theorist of the *neue typographie*). In this role he became the linchpin of graphic reform under the Weimar Republic. With the advent of Nazism, in the critical year of 1933, Renner was suspended and then dismissed from his post, although not before he had organized (in March and May) German participation in the 5th Milan Triennale in the name of the Berlin Werkbund. Here he mounted—under the watchful eye of a brownshirt—an exhibition devoted to the graphic arts and industries, for which he ironically received a grand diploma of honor and the official recognition of the authorities, commencing with a visit from the king. Renner survived the Nazi years in a sort of "internal exile," although he remained active both as designer and writer. (It is worth singling out, in an extensive bibliography, his 1940 book *Die Kunst der Typographie*, a reverse echo of his earlier *Typographie als Kunst*, published in 1922, as well as the "progressive" *Mechanisierte Grafik* of 1931). He began to make his presence felt as a critic again in the debates of the postwar years, as the voice of bitter experience and reason, in a slow decline that culminated in his death in 1956. So Burke's book on Renner is a work of fundamental importance. Perhaps he can be criticized for not having paid enough attention, amidst so much research in the archives, to the episode of the Triennale, ignoring the documentation available and the profound impact that Renner's exhibition had on Italian graphics. It is no coincidence that 1933 was the year of the reform of *Casabella* (with the new masthead composed in Futura, just as it is today), the birth of *Campo grafico* and the beginning of the activity of the Boggeri studio, to mention only a few significant developments. Burke has also overlooked the considerable interest taken by the Italian press. (He would have found it useful to consult at least Guido Modiano, "Tipografia di Edoardo Persico," in *Campo grafico*, 1935, 11–12). Edoardo Persico wrote about the event in *L'Italia letteraria* for May 1933, concluding prophetically: "At the Milan Triennale only the German exhibition, which was confined to samples of graphic art, and the Swedish exhibition … are abreast of European taste. It suffices to note how typographical composition in Germany seeks a balance and rhythm that exists independently of the contents of the writing to understand that this graphic expressionism embodies the most vital style of modern architecture... In 1936 we may not be seeing in Milan either Paul Renner, who has organized this exhibition of German printing, nor any of his fellow countrymen who have brought about the revolution in modern architecture."

F₁ DIE GEEIGNETE SCHRIFT

FUTURA

in allen Größen

und allen Schnitten, für alle Zwecke.

mager	4 - 84 Punkt
halbfett	4 - 84 Punkt
dreiviertelfett	6 - 84 Punkt
fett	6 - 84 Punkt
black	20 - 84 Punkt
schräg mager	6 - 48 Punkt
schräg halbfett	6 - 48 Punkt
schmalfett	6 - 84 Punkt
PLAKAT halbfett	8 - 60 Cicero
PLAKAT fett	8 - 60 Cicero
PLAKAT schmalfett	8 - 60 Cicero
PLAKAT black	8 - 60 Cicero

Bauersche Gießerei · Frankfurt am Main

Gezeichnet von Paul Renner, München

12

DIE GEEIGNETE SCHRIFT F₁

FUTURA

ihre Vorzüge:

konstruktiv und bestimmt im Ausdruck,

klar, exakte Formen, gleichmäßiger Lauf, schmucklos,

elegant, rassig, klassisch rein, edel, ebenmäßig in den Verhältnissen, abstrakte Strenge,

neutral, große Ruhe des Satzbildes, lebendig im Versalsatz, vielseitig,

leicht lesbar, Betonung formaler Gegensätze der einzelnen Buchstaben, knapp, präzis,

gespannt, bewegt charaktervoll, technisch,

geistreich, trotz des sauberen Stils der Maschine; daher suggestiv.

NICHT DAS KLEINE α

unterscheidet die Futura wesentlich, **sondern ihre Gestalt, ihr Reichtum, ihre Durcharbeit.**

13

The Century...The Broadway...The Overland...The Golden State...Four of the dozens of superb trains operated daily over American Railroads. • To express these four and their many sisters, in type as powerful, as clean cut, as distinguished as the trains themselves, has hitherto been rather a problem. • With FUTURA BOLD, however, conveying the same energetic, abstract and logical qualities, this problem fades to the vanishing point. • Never was there a type face better suited to present the message of not only the railroads but also the entire heavy industries, than this...

FUTURA
the type of today
and tomorrow

THE BAUER TYPE FOUNDRY, INC., NEW YORK
At Two-Thirty-Five East Forty-Fifth Street

previous pages: Paul Renner (Wernigerode 1878, Munich 1956) in a photograph by E. Wasow, 1930.
left: text set in 8.5/11 pt. *Futura*.
above: *Die neue Gestaltung in der Typographie*, two plates from Kurt Schwitters' booklet, 1930 (p. 102).
left: *Futura the type of today and tomorrow*, advertisement for the Bauer Type Foundry carried by the annual publication of the Art Directors Club of New York, 1930.

125

above: *For Photomontage Futura and Futura the Script of Our Time Accompanies the Image of Our Time*, full-page advertisements for the marketing of Paul Renner's typeface, 1927. below: the letters "c" and "a," mirrored, superimposed and inscribed in a circle, reveal the quantity of corrections that render *Futura* a balanced typeface suitable for running text. It is no coincidence that Edoardo Persico (1900–36) adopted it, between 1933 and 1934, for his extraordinary redesign of the magazine *Casabella*; compare with p. 99 and p. 114.

FUTURA
die Schrift unserer Zeit
BEGLEITE
das Bild unserer Zeit

IBM

r

If we exclude from the literature on Rand what is, after all not, a very bountiful crop of articles in various magazines and periodicals (few of them, in any case, of much significance), until quite recently the only studies of Rand's work were the ones he wrote himself. While certainly not negligible, these are inevitably self-referential and semi-autobiographical and need to be viewed largely in their documentary value and as the "symptoms" of a poetic.

Recently the gap has been filled by a luxurious large-format volume from the skilled pen of Steven Heller. Heller has not only distinguished himself for his copious output in the American literature specializing in graphics; he is also senior art director of the *New York Times*, editor of the *AIGA Journal of Graphic Design* and a professor in the Master of Fine Arts Illustration program at the School of Visual Arts in New York—a true authority as well as a prolific one in this field. His book is entitled simply and without further ado *Paul Rand* (how could it be otherwise?). This authentic coffee-table book, whose physical weight by itself demands attention, is published by the Phaidon Press (London 1999) and includes in its over 250 pages a short preface by Armin Hofmann, a slightly longer introduction by George Lois and a final chapter on the teachings of Rand as "modern professor" by Jessica Helf and, followed by the customary and useful chronology and bibliography.

Accompanied by a lavish, extremely well-chosen and striking set of illustrations, Heller's text forms the body of the volume. It is divided into five chapters, which correspond roughly to the phases of Rand's career. We discover that our man, who was born in 1914 along with a twin brother named Fishel (who died very young) to a family of strict orthodox Jews and grew up in the Brownsville district of Brooklyn, New York, was actually called Peretz Rosenbaum and later adopted the pseudonym of Paul Rand because of its less "ethnic" connotations. After studying (1929–32) first at the Pratt Institute and then at the Parsons School of Design, Rand went on to take a course in drawing from George Grosz in 1933. His first significant works date from the mid-thirties: art director (1936–41) of the magazines *Apparel Arts* and *Esquire*, his designs included an outstanding series of covers for *Direction* (1938–45). Rand's work was soon noticed by Laszlo Moholy-Nagy, who published one of the very first articles about him in 1941. In the same year, at the age of twenty-seven, Rand became art director of one of the most important advertising agencies in New York, William H. Weintraub, where he worked until 1955, creating some memorable campaigns (one example will serve for all: the ads for El Producto cigars). He was also active in the field of publishing (magazine and book covers, in particular for Knopf). In 1946 he published his first book, *Thoughts on Design* (reprinted in 1970), followed, between 1985 and 1996, by *Paul Rand. A Designer's Art, Design, Form, and Chaos: From Lascaux to Brooklyn.*

Quickly scaling the heights of American graphics, in the mid-fifties Rand embarked on a series of extremely long-lasting consultancies

Paul Rand

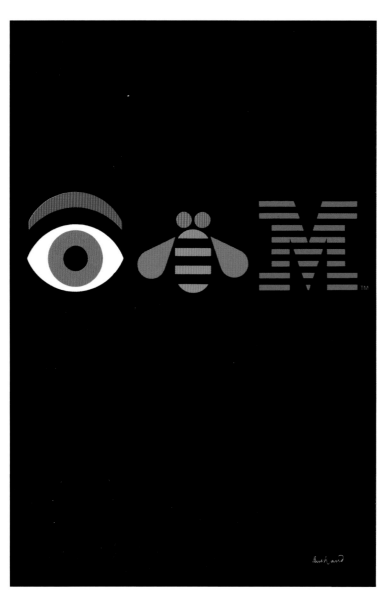

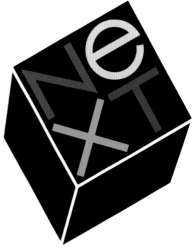

("good design is good business") for the corporate identity of several industrial giants, which made him famous: IBM (1959–91), Westinghouse (1959–81) and Cummins (1961–96). And then there were his other logos, masterpieces of copybook design, from UPS (1961) and ABC (1962) to NeXT (1986) and USSB (1995). The model to which he looked in his first engagement with IBM was the publicity material of the Italian firm Olivetti, which also commissioned Rand to design some posters for Marcello Nizzoli's legendary Lettera 22 typewriter.

Despite his many other commitments, in all these years Rand still found time to teach, at first occasionally and then regularly, at some prestigious schools, such as Yale, Harvard (1956–69, 1974–96), and Brissago (1977–96), right up till his death in 1996. Extremely accurate though with a tendency toward hagiography in its text, ably supplemented by extracts from interviews with various collaborators, Steven Heller's book-testimonial on Paul Rand is a title that was missing from the specialist literature. In many ways it finally fills a gap on our shelves that could not be justified, except by care and commitment needed to carry out such an undertaking.

previous pages: Paul Rand (New York 1914, Norwalk 1996), n.d.
Some of the logotypes he created: IBM, 1962; ABC, 1962; Cummins, 1962; Ford, 1966; Yale University Press, 1985; USSB, 1995.
left: IBM, poster, 1981: although a champion of the logotype as the cornerstone of the corporate image and theorist of its prescriptive use, Paul Rand reinterprets the *IBM* logotype in a phonetic-visual key in this case: I (eye) B (bee) M (letter "m"): the letter "m" confers recognizability on the logotypal rebus, the eye conveys the idea of measure, the bee that of industriousness; themes already encountered on p. 83 and p. 53 (*AEG* honeycomb logotype, 1908).
bottom left: *Next*, logotype, 1986; "the most expensive logotype in history," for a computer that was too advanced for the market.
left: Westinghouse, animation of the logotype, 1960–62.

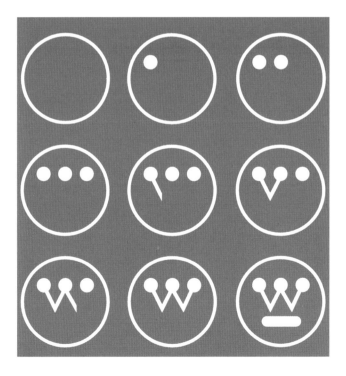

131

wolfgang weingart from nieuwe beelding to new wave

In the years between the two World Wars a complex and seldom explored historical path led to the formation in Germany of a distinctively systematic approach to graphics. It favored informative rigor, economy of means, socio-communicative aims, and the creation of universal languages rather than a taste for expression, artistic indulgences, games played with form or personal lines of research. This is the phenomenon that was later, after a favorable period of incubation in Switzerland, to become commonly known as Swiss graphics, and which developed into a sort of visual International Style. It held sway all the whole world from the fifties to the seventies and is still used today in certain circles.

Obliged by the tyranny of space to neglect other fundamental contributions (such as those of Otto Neurath or Kurt Schwitters, not to mention Herbert Bayer, Laszlo Moholy-Nagy or El Lissitzky, among others), we would at least like to present here—very succinctly, through a few outstanding episodes—the significant outline of this history, as we see it. It takes some quite unexpected turns.

Nieuwe Beelding > 1922

A key figure at De Stijl, the vehicle for the diffusion of the ascetic abstraction of Dutch Nieuwe Beelding (neoplasticism), the brilliant cultural propagandist C.E.M. Küpper—better known as Theo van Doesburg—taught a polemical course at Weimar, aimed at demonstrating to teachers and students of the Bauhaus the "principles of a new and radical creative process" and the results of an "exact" chromoplastic approach to artistic problems. Among those who took the course were Max Burchartz, Werner Gräff and Peter Röhl, students at the Bauhaus with a background in painting, including recent incursions into Expressionism, and an artistic vocation and training. For them, it was a sort of conversion on the road to Weimar. Shortly afterward they were all professionally engaged in the design of graphics, based on systematic principles, for public and private bodies.

1923
Gräff developed his *Material zum Problem einer Internationalen Verkehrs-Zeichen-Sprache*, a project for an international set of road signs based on the use of color and standardized lettering.

1926
Röhl presented an even more radical standardization of signs, with a universal family of pictograms for public places.

1924 / 27
Giving up his work as a painter and artist, Burchartz (Johannes Canis's partner in the werbe-bau graphics studio at Bochum in 1924–27), designed one of the first systematic examples of signage for a building, based on the use of color, in Alfred Fischer's Hans-Sachs-Haus at Gelsenkirchen (1924–27). At the same time, Burchartz's ideas about advertising design, "Gestaltung der Reklame," published in *Die Form* in 1926 but known already since 1924, proved exceptionally important in the history of contemporary visual

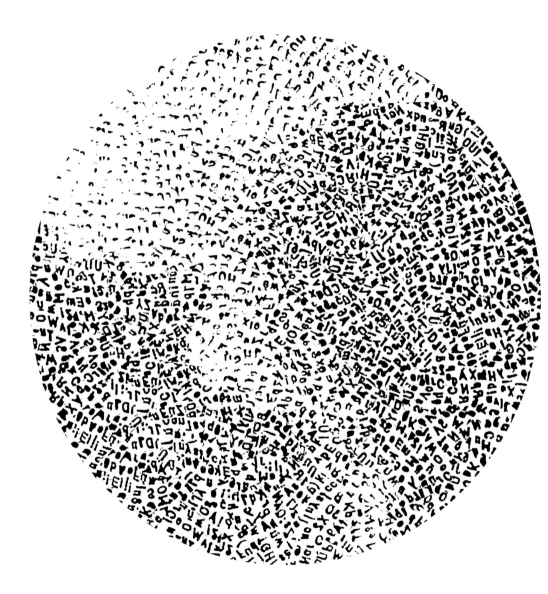

134

design. In *Graphic Design. A Concise History* (London 1994), perhaps the finest historical outline of modern graphic design, Richard Hollis writes: "In a long article Burchartz analyses the function of publicity, what makes it effective, and how the viewer is involved. The concept of message and receiver, which became a common way of looking at communication in the 1950s, was introduced. But the larger part of Burchatz's essay is devoted to 'The aesthetic organization of the means of the advertising medium'... These principles Burchartz worked out in the designs that established the style of International Modernism, which survived Nazism to re-emerge in the 1960s as the 'Swiss style.'"

1927 / 29

The cities of Bochum and Dortmund, for the first time in history, hired graphic artists to design all their printed material and create a distinctive public identity. The designers were, respectively, Anton Stankowski (who studied under Burchartz at the Folkwangschule in Essen in 1927–29 and was also a freelance collaborator with the Canis agency in Bochum) in 1927, and Burchartz in 1929.

1929

Moving to Switzerland, Stankowski worked at the Agentur Max Dalang in Zurich until 1937. He was a true pioneer of industrial graphics, the exact opposite of the graphics of illustration. He emphasized simplicity, asymmetry, freedom of composition and exclusive use of the Akzidenz Grotesk sans serif font.

1933

Jan Tschichold, subversive promoter of asymmetrical graphics, "Bolshevik" advocate of *elementare typographie* (1925) and author of the renowned *Die neue Typographie* (1928), emigrated from Nazi Germany (after he and his wife had been held in "protective custody" for six weeks) and sought refuge in Basel . There he took a controversial turn toward tradition, making Switzerland his second home (living there until 1974, apart from a period in London in 1946–49).

1939 / 45

During the war, in the neutral Swiss Confederation, all these seeds sprouted in the fertile local ground, hybridizing with indigenous ones (Max Bill, Cyliax, Walter Herdeg, Herbert Matter, Emil Schulthess, Alfred Willimann and others), with close links to Concrete Art and the "Abstraction-Création. Art non figuratif" movement.

1946

After the students at the Allgemeine Kunstgewerbeschule in Basel reprinted some masterworks of twenties graphics under the guidance of Emil Ruder, a violent dispute broke out between Bill and Tschichold over the significance of modernity in graphics, the former seeing it as a progressive-transgressive factor, the latter as a realistic-reflective one.

1955

Karl Gestner, a graphic artist in Basel (in partnership with Markus Kutter), who was held up as an example of innovative capacity by

previous pages: Wolfgang Weingart (Salemertal, 1941) in a recent photograph by Melchior Imboden. left: Circular Composition, reproduction of the print of a free assemblage of typefaces, front, 1962–63; the transversal and deconstructive use of the traditional materials of the typographer (leads, screens, films) is characteristic of the work and teaching of Wolfgang Weingart.

right: *Visible Language*, cover
design for the magazine,
superimposition of collage
and screens manipulated
in the darkroom, 1974–76.
following pages: *Circular
Composition*, reproduction
of the print of a free
assemblage of typefaces,
back, 1962–63.

Bill, designed and laid out an important monographic issue of *Werk*
devoted to graphics. It illustrated the "persuasive" side of graphics
with the work of the Zurich-based studio Odermatt & Tissi: this
provided the opportunity to develop a *sachlich* concept of the "grid"
as the framework of order and regulation in the design of printed
matter.

1957

Max Miedinger was commissioned by Edouard Hoffmann to design
a sans serif font for the Swiss foundry Haas. Called the Neue Haas
Grotesk, based on the Akzidenz Grotesk so highly appreciated by
Stankowski, it was destined for worldwide fame and success. For
distribution on the German market, by Stempel in 1961, it was renamed (*omen nomen*) Helvetica, a typeface all too familiar to everyone.

1958

Publication began of the trilingual Swiss magazine *Neue Grafik* with
the aim of "creating an international base for the discussion of modern graphics and the applied arts," the result of uncompromising
commitment by the "gang of four": Richard P. Lohse (also responsible for a fundamental book on exhibition design); Josef Müller-Brockmann (author, among other standard texts, of *Gestaltungsprobleme
des Grafikers*, the first systematic codification of the *Raster Systeme*);
Hans Neuburg, collaborator of Stankowski; Carlo Vivarelli, collaborator of Antonio Boggeri.

1967

"It was in the Basel and Zurich design schools," explains Hollis
again, in the abovementioned volume," that the Swiss style ... was
consolidated and developed. In the 1970s and 1980s established
designers ... and a new generation of brilliant poster designers
built on it freely. They adapted their methods to each job, without
restricting themselves to Akzidenz and Helvetica, and the recti-
linear layouts that had typified the style. Akzidenz, particularly in
its boldest version, was nevertheless the preferred typeface of
Wolfgang Weingart, the most influential younger Swiss designer
abroad ... Since 1967, he had enjoyed a role as enfant terrible,
enthusiastically questioning received attitudes and demonstrating
his own in a considerable output of experimental work. His mouth-
piece was the monthly *Typographische Monatsblätter*, whose covers
(fifteen in 1972 and 1973) ... were designed to take the reader 'step
by step through a terminology as defined by various design theoreti-
cians and communication scientists ... the composition ignores
hand-setting dogma and challenges design ideology.' Weingart
toured the United States in 1972 and 1973. He published his
lecture in 1976, entitled *How Can One Make Swiss Typography
Work?*, which was concerned mainly with the teaching at Basel...
Weingart moved graphics into the realm of personal expression,
which reached an extreme in his cover design for the American
academic journal *Visible Language* in 1974, where he scrawled

d design. Undoubtedly, design criteria are
perticinly, remain independent; namely, t
rography, its design criteria, how one defi
mmunications' goal, message, medium, an

fragt sich, wie es mit seiner Typografie w
Art, wie er diese Frage – den gesamten T
utet er bereits die Antwort an.

'No idea for this fucking cover today.' But Weingart's significance is in his early recognition of a new technology ... He met this challenge with inventive gusto, exploiting phototypesetting and the use of photographic film to collage alphabet and images."

Weingart was invited to teach at Basel by Armin Hofmann (also a visiting professor at the Philadelphia Museum School of Art and Yale University since the fifties). In the introduction to the English edition of the lecture cited above, Weingart described this period: "In 1968, when I started to teach at the Basel School of Design in Switzerland, it was clear that I had to expand radically the thoughts, theories and visual restrictions of so-called 'Swiss Typography' ... I am basically self-taught. This made it possible for me to be free of design trends, movements, or styles. However, the kind of freedom I created for myself requires strict discipline and a sense of responsibility ... At that time, almost twenty years ago, no one thought this new visual attitude and method of experimentation could be the beginning of today's so-called 'New Wave' style. During the past two decades there have been students from about twenty-five different countries in our advanced class of graphic design. These former students are now scattered all over the continents."

So the standardizing American New Wave, the digital hybrid imagery first described by April Greiman and the visual deconstructivism of the United States had their roots in old Europe, and above all perhaps in Weingart's radical critique of a "Swiss graphics" that had been reduced to empty stylistic features. In the eighties the New Wave fed on (sometimes poorly digested) ideas from the Old World, before spreading everywhere in the nineties: from California (where Greiman, a student of Weingart's in Basel, quickly attracted attention, along with Lucille Tenazas, David Carson, who had studied graphics in Switzerland and, above all, the European émigrés Rudy van der Lans and Zuzana Licko); from the Cranbrook Academy of Art (thanks to the many years of joint activity by the McCoys); from MIT (with the seminal Visible Language Workshop of Muriel Cooper, editor of *Visible Language*); from Yale (the teaching base of Dan Friedman, a student at Basel and Ulm, the organizer of Weingart's first American tour and the author of *Radical Modernism*); and from New York (with the "undesign," for example, of Tibor Kalman—later the editor of *Colors*—and M&Co, the cold style of Willi Kunz and the Dutch taste of Doublespace—a duo formed at Cranbrook).

In its long march, propelled by a wind from the north, Swiss graphics, overcoming its own crisis after the past era of imperial dominion, dared to turn its prow again toward the New World, and returned to conquer the West.

1987 > New Wave

max huber notes on concrete abstraction

Max Huber was born in 1919 at Baar (Zug), a citizen of the Swiss Confederation, a country with one of the most distinguished records in graphic design in the second half of the 20th century. A native Swiss-German speaker, Max attended elementary and high school at Baar. From a very early age he displayed a particular flair for the visual arts—during summer vacations at Mühlehorn (Glarus), for instance, he fascinated the customers at his grandparents' inn with drawings traced in chalk on the big table with its slate top. Finishing the Gymnasium (high school) in Baar, he enrolled in the Kunstgewerbeschule in Zurich in 1935. One of the students at the school was Werner Bischof, a pioneer of "objective" photographic research, with whom Max soon made friends, following him in his experiments. But the real pillar in the young Huber's intellectual formation was one of the teachers in the preparatory course, Alfred Willimann, instructor in graphics and photo-graphics, who introduced him to contemporary culture in all its diversity, in particular to the avant-garde, from El Lissitzky to Jan Tschichold. Thus it was Willimann who directed Huber's creative powers into the channel of ideas in which they were to develop, steering him toward a rigorous form of visual culture capable of nurturing and guiding his research. Willimann was himself a prominent figure in contemporary Swiss culture, as an artist and member since 1932 of "Abstraction-Création," a sort of Internationale of the nonrepresentational, the geometric-constructive art whose roots lay in the most radically "abstract" movements of the Netherlands and the Soviet Union between the end of the teens and the twenties.

In this connection, it is worth recalling, if only in passing, that shortly before he died, at the end of a long, difficult and sometimes contradictory career as the key figure in De Stijl and Dutch neoplasticism, C.E.M. Küpper (better known as Theo van Doesburg) founded the magazine *Art Concret* in Paris in 1930. Only the introductory issue came out. The ideas presented in this umpteenth, little known and perhaps misunderstood effort by the brilliant Dutch practitioner of agitprop was to be pondered over the next two decades, with effects that were spread beyond Europe. Art should "strive towards absolute clarity," explains the manifesto, namely towards "concrete and not abstract painting, for there is nothing more concrete, more real, than a line, a color, a plane... The development of painting is nothing but the intellectual search for truth through visual culture..." Painting is a medium for the visualization of thought: every picture is a thought-color because "there is nothing to read in painting. Only to see." The same year, the French artist and critic Michel Seuphor, friend and biographer of Piet Mondrian, founded another group in Paris with an equally programmatic name, Cercle et Carré, in open opposition to van Doesburg but with intentions that were not very different. In 1931 the two efforts were combined, in a sense, with the birth of *Abstraction-Création. Art non figuratif*, a periodical and a

**On the trail
of the young Max**

Abstract art, concrete art

previous pages: Max Huber
(Baar 1919, Mendrisio 1992),
left, and Achille Castiglioni,
right, wearing *Record*
watches on their wrists, 1989.
La Rinascente logotype, 1950.
left: *Photographic Self-Portrait*,
1940 and *Photogram*, 1941.
bottom left: graphics of Achille
and Pier Giacomo Castiglioni's
display *The Developments
of the Petrochemical Industry
through the History of the Drop
of Oil*, 1964.
above and left: *Borsalino*,
postcards, 1949–50.

8th Milan Triennale,
poster, 1947.
7th CIAM Bergamo, poster,
1949; observe the insistent
use of Grotesk typefaces
in both posters, connecting
the work of Max Huber with
the schools of Zurich and
Basel.
Personal visiting card, 1939
the theme of the spiral band
recurs several times in
Max Huber's designs (p. 143
and is the central element
of the cover of a promotiona
brochure for the Studio
Boggeri of 1940.

cosmopolitan and varied group that included many of the nonfigurative artists present in Paris—Kandinsky, Mondrian, Pevsner, Gabo, Arp, Schwitters, Nicholson, Moholy-Nagy, Kupka, Delaunay, Albers, Magnelli, Herbin and Hélion, to mention only the foremost —as well as a large number of associates throughout Europe and beyond, until the members exceeded four hundred (before it disbanded in 1936). Thirteen of them were Swiss, including Sophie Taeuber-Arp, Max Bill and Willimann, Max's first teacher.

From Zurich to Milan...

To return to Max. Rather than go to work at the spinning mill in Baar, as his family could no longer keep him at the Kunstgewerbeschule, he managed to get himself taken on in 1936 as an apprentice graphic artist at the P.O. Althaus agency in Zurich, where he soon found himself working with Gerard Miedinger and Emil Schulthess. As an apprentice, moreover, he was obliged to attend school one day a week, where he continued to study under Willimann. Also in 1936, the exhibition "Zeitprobleme in der Schweizer Malerei und Skulptur" was held at the Kunsthaus in Zurich, which must have provided Max with more than a little food for thought—especially in view of the fact that the catalogue carried an essay by Max Bill with the significant title "Concrete Design," fully in keeping with the position of van Doesburg. Shortly afterward, in 1939, Schulthess gave the young Max his big break, hiring him as his assistant for makeup at Conzett+Huber, an important publisher in Zurich. In those years Conzett+Huber published two avant-garde periodicals that took a progressive stand with which Max sympathized. Edited by Arnold Kübler, both periodicals had Schulthess as art director. They were the weekly ZI. *Zürcher Illustrierte* (which closed a few years later), the first magazine with four-color reproductions in Switzerland, and the monthly *DU*, to which the photographer Werner Bischof also contributed. Drafted into the Swiss army in 1939, Max found himself serving alongside Bischof for a while; at the same time he got to know Bill, Neuburg and Müller-Brockmann when on leave. So continued the series of meetings and friendships with leading figures that were a feature of his curious and attentive attitude to life, in a spirit open to innovation and the most diverse encounters.
In 1940 he found out through *DU* that the most important and accomplished communications agency in Italy, the Boggeri studio in Milan, was looking for a graphic designer. Getting temporary leave of absence from the army to go abroad, Max knocked at Boggeri's door in February 1940; he hardly knew a word of Italian but he had the reckless confidence in himself and his abilities that only a twenty-year-old can (and should) have.
Antonio Boggeri was a cultivated man with an international outlook unusual in Fascist Italy and a true professional of communication. From the thirties to the seventies he brought together many of the best names in Italian graphics (such as Erberto Carboni, Bruno Munari, Remo Muratore, Marcello Nizzoli, Imre Reiner and Xanti Schawinsky,

... and back again

in the prewar alone). He created an innovative atmosphere with integrated production and working methods. He was well placed to judge who he was dealing with: a simple test, the sketch of a visiting card, sufficed to show him what Max was made of. Despite his youth and an experience that, however distinguished, was limited, Boggeri immediately entrusted him with tasks of great responsibility in the studio, as well as allowing him considerable creative freedom.

Equally immediate for Max was the discovery of the Milanese milieu best suited to his interests and his thirst for knowledge. He rapidly made the acquaintance of key figures such as Franco Albini and BBPR, Giovanni Pintori and Albe Steiner, Saul Steinberg and Luigi Veronesi. In many cases, these encounters led to relations of esteem and friendship: with Albe and Lica Steiner, for instance, he began to collaborate on the layout of the house organ of Bemberg, a major textile manufacturer, and embarked on visual experiments of various kinds. So in addition to his graphic work, Max continued the wide-ranging development, as assiduous as it was independent, that was his distinctive quality. For instance, he improved his drawing technique at the Brera Academy and put his aptitude for objective vision to the test by exploring photography, as shown by a series of pictures of a silent and deserted Milan or an extraordinary self-portrait taken in 1940: it presents a young man with immature features but a determined expression in a convincing if not original photogrammatic construction.

Just a few months after Max's arrival in Milan, in June 1940, Fascist Italy went to war totally unprepared. His work, increasingly interesting and demanding, encountered the difficulties of the wartime climate: to cut a long story short, Max was obliged to return to Zurich in 1941. He was immediately called up, but in 1942 was already able to go back to work at Conzett+Huber, where he collaborated with Schulthess at *DU*, while often acting as an assistant to Bischof, on both photography and exhibition design. He also designed posters, theatrical scenery and murals. Through Bill, in the tragic (even in neutral Switzerland) years of the war, he intensified his contacts with the artistic circles in Zurich that he found most congenial, those of Hans Arp, Camille Graeser, Leo Leuppi and Richard Paul Lohse. He took part in the activities of the Allianz Vereinigung moderner Schweizer Künstler and various other initiatives, such as the magazine *abstract/konkret* (1944–45), with close affinities to his own ideas. His studio above the Schauspielhaus was a meeting place for theatrical characters, such as Theo Otto, as well as Italian exiles, such as Ignazio Silone or Franco Fortini. In 1945, as soon as the war was over, Max crossed the border from Vacallo to Como in secret and returned to Milan, where he at once started working with Boggeri again. He sought out his old friends and made new ones, like Luigi Longo or Gabriele Mucchi and his wife Genni. Through Steiner, he met Elio Vittorini (later contributing to his *Il Politecnico*) and Giulio Einaudi.

Gran premio dell'Autodromo

dell'Autodromo

17 ottobre 1948

Monza

12° gran premio

21 giugno 1970 · ore 15.30

della Lotteria di Monza

Automobile Club Milano · Patrocinio AGIP

previous page: *Grand Prix
at the Monza Racing Track*,
poster, 1948.
above: *12th Monza Grand Prix
Lottery*, poster, 1970.

In 1946 Giulio Einaudi, the most important cultural publisher in Italy, commissioned him to renew the typography of his publishing house, providing him with a studio and home at the firms offices in Milan. During the weekly meetings at the head office in Turin, Max got to know Italo Calvino, Natalia Ginzburg, Massimo Mila, Cesare Pavese, Fernanda Pivano, Stefano Terra—in short, he mixed with the Italian left-wing intellectuals and artists. He soon came into contact with Birolli, Cassinari, Consagra, Dorazio, Fontana, Guttuso, Perilli and Turcato. In 1947 he worked on a memorable series of exhibitions: a traveling exhibition on the Resistance in Italy (with Remo Muratore, whom he had met in 1940), one on the socialist newspaper *Avanti* (with Paolo Grassi), another devoted to abstract and concrete art, for which he also designed the graphics. In the same year, the tour de force, with his pupil Ezio Bonini, of the image of the 8th Milan Triennale (printing materials and signs), which he succinctly renamed T8, in collaboration with Piero Bottoni.

The year 1948 saw him increasingly busy: he worked with the BBPR studio on the project for the Terni pavilion at the Milan Trade Fair; he began a long collaboration with the Castiglioni brothers, with an exhibition devoted to Radio Newscasts for the RAI, the Italian public service broadcaster. For the international festival of contemporary music at the Venice Biennale, at the request of the maestro Ferdinando Ballo (whom he had met that year along with the critic Roberto Leydi), he designed the graphics and the scenery for *L'incubo* at La Fenice opera house. He won first prize in the competition for the poster for the Monza Grand Prix, with a design (reminiscent of Moholy-Nagy) that he was able to skillfully ring the changes on for years; he taught at the Rinascita school, alongside Albe Steiner, Gabrieke Mucchi and Luigi Veronesi.

In 1949 an important conference of the CIAM (the International Congresses of Modern Architecture founded in 1928) was held in Bergamo. Max did the graphics for the event and had the opportunity to meet Le Corbusier, Aldo van Eyck and other leading modern architects. The same year W.H. Sandberg, director of the Stedelijk Museum in Amsterdam and a graphic artist of exceptional talent, asked Max to send him some of his posters for the museum's collection, a sign of the fact that his fame had now spread beyond the borders of his adopted country and reached institutions interested in the culture of images. The rest of the story is well-known, even to those only vaguely familiar with the course of European graphic design after the war.

Max is internationally recognized as one of the outstanding figures from the end of the forties (when we shall stop dogging his footsteps), down to the late seventies at least, with paradigmatic attainments in graphic design, including exhibition installations (especially with the Castiglioni brothers), corporate design and advertising. At the end of the sixties, Max returned to the Canton Ticino in Switzerland.

The years of reconstruction

Thinking in images

43rd Italian Grand Prix Monza
Racing Track, poster, 1972.

His work was consistently brilliant and fascinating, never predictable; he achieved subtle balances through a predilection for experiment and risk; it was fluid and elegant in the relationship between images and words, neither subservient to the other nor reduced to mere function.

Huber's work intermeshed the different fields in which he used his creative talents: his multi-faceted graphic designs, painting, photography and other visual media form a creative continuum that can hardly be reduced to the specifics of any one field of experiment. And, even confining ourselves to the graphic designs that made him justly famous, we should not overlook his undisputed gifts as a book designer (with the series for Einaudi, for example) or his fundamental contribution to the systematic graphics of "corporate images." He designed historic logotypes for La Rinascente and Coin (department stores) and Esselunga (a supermarket chain), and worked with artists of the caliber of Braendli, Legler and Nava. In the introduction to a monograph on his work at in the early, Max chose to emphasize the broad, though not indiscriminate, experimental range of his work, and named his principal influences: Bayer, El Lissitzky, Heartfield, Matter, Moholy-Nagy, Neuburg, Schuitema, Stankowski, Sutnar, Tschichold, Willimann and Zwart.

Max's work needs to be seen in these comprehensive terms, with its empirical striving towards abstraction that became a concrete exploration of the "powers" of the visual arts and the very concept of Gestalt. With experimental coherence he tackled the design of everyday items, practical objects and forms of communication. Significantly, he often used interacting patterns based on a generative figure like the spiral to express the cochlear expansion of the randomness of life into the regularities of form. His work was an attempt (limited, perhaps uneven, but certainly tangible and useful) to give form at least to the splinters of a noble dream, to present the fragments of a utopia that had inspired one of the most radical and fascinating currents in the 20th-century artistic avant-garde: one that sought the death of art and its replacement by a broad aesthetic quality that would pervade the whole of life and the environment. This obliges us to take a less sectorial and more flexible approach to the contribution that he and other graphic artists made to the contemporary mode for "thinking in images," and to imagine a history of Bildhafte Denken that has yet to be written.

adrian frutiger petite histoire de l'univers

This could be sub-subtitled: notes towards a nonlinear history of the linear. Better still: fluctuations of the linear. Because what the French subtitle alludes to is not the infinite universe of cosmology, of philosophy, of belles-lettres: neither what "produces all things, and governs all things" (Anaximander), nor "a movement to go ever further" (Malebranche), nor even the "idea capable of corrupting all others" (Borges). Prosaically (to the letter), it is a typeface, universally (to make a joke of it) known as Univers. It is a sans serif: a "type of character without terminal lines (> Serif) that is inspired by the linear letters of the Greek alphabet and those of the archaic Roman," succinctly explains the entry in Giorgio Fioravanti's *Il dizionario del grafico* (Zanichelli, Bologna 1993). The cross-reference tells us: "Serif. Terminal line of a letter of the alphabet (> Character). The form of the serif is decisive in distinguishing the design of a character and in giving it a classification."

Adrian Frutiger
(Unterseen 1928)

Question: how do we distinguish and classify linear fonts, lacking serifs—but not, one hopes, lacking grace—by definition? We can consult the dictionary again, looking at the correlated entries. (An idea strikes me: could the dictionary be the stepmother of all those hypertexts we hear so much about?). In the end, the impression we get is that the science of type is an uncertain typology; *sotto voce*: confidential sources hint at interesting works in progress on the subject in Italy, a country not new to undertakings of the kind.

The fact is that the classical taxonomies of Thibaudeau (1924), Vox (1954), Novarese (1956) and Pellitteri (1958), as well as the DIN 16518 classification (1964), waver between vague stylistic features, imprecise pseudo-historic periodizations and summary and partial descriptions. They tell us nothing, for instance, about the Gestalt, the overall essential conformation of the letters, the "A-ness of As," as Matthew Carter would put it. Nothing of what the *esprit de finesse* of a Roland Barthes has to suggest, for instance, about the typology: "In a single cultural or historical field, modes of writing break away from or are generated by others," he declares in "Variations sur l'écriture" (*Le Plaisir du texte*, Seuil, Paris 2000). "They are often opposed, because of their function… But equally often, in our history, types of writing based on simple differentiations of form—differences that are in a way not necessary but from which it is possible to derive, by counterpoint, this or that ethical implication—come together… To conclude, writing, like any historical phenomenon, is overdetermined: it seems to be the product, at one and the same time, of material factors (writing gets smaller if it is necessary to save space, when the support is expensive) and spiritual motivations (writing is shaved to bring it closer to the style of an era and, if I may be permitted this, to 'prove' that there is a philosophy of History: i.e. that there is one and only one History)."

However this may be, the genealogy of our Univers extends back to classical antiquity. Without venturing too far into the paleographic literature (where Italy excels), confirmation of this can already be found in Nicolete Gray's magnum opus, *A History of Lettering* (Phaidon, London

1986): in the epigraphy of Greece and republican Rome the letters are often linear.

Continuing our research, though by leaps and bounds, we discover that, in the essay "Sans Serif and Other Experimental Inscribed Lettering of the Early Renaissance" (in *Motif*, 5, 1960, reprinted in abstract by Letterperfect, Seattle 1997), Gray discusses the Humanistic revival of the sans serif in the works of Lorenzo Ghiberti, Donatello, Michelozzo, Luca della Robbia and Bernardo Rossellino: not to speak of Alberti (going down this road, we come to Alvar Aalto...).

Moreover, in the recent, and excellent, *The Nymph and the Grot. The Revival of the Sanserif Letter* (Friends of the St. Bride Printing Library, London 1999), such a genuine authority as James Mosley investigates an umpteenth variation of linear, modern this time. He points to scrolls in drawings by George Dance Jr. and John Soane, as well as the work of Thomas Banks and John Flaxman, and so arrives at the first of the sans serif typefaces, the Two Lines English Egyptian of William Caslon IV (circa 1819). But there are also those, in Italy, who have conjectured the existence of a different path, which starts from Piranesi.

And Univers? We're almost there. A further revival of the sans serif took place at the turn of the 19th century. Good examples are fonts like Akzidenz-Grotesk (1898) or News Gothic (1908), the typeface used for this book. Another linear wave, in the first and second decade of the 20th century, came with types like London Underground (1916), Erbar (1924), Kabel (1927), Futura (1927) and Gill Sans (1927), flanked by the experiments of De Stijl and the Bauhaus.

This brings us down to the present. When the young Swiss typographer Adrian Frutiger, a graduate of the school of applied arts in Zurich, went to work at the Parisian foundry of Deberny & Peignot, he soon found himself having to redesign historic typefaces for the first efficient phototypesetter, the American Photon. Charles Peignot, licensee of the Photon (called Lumitype in France), wanted a sans serif font designed specially for the machine that would revolutionize printing, killing off lead type. This was not long before the third linear revival of the 20th century, with Helvetica (1957) and Optima (1958) as "first among equals." Drawing on formal exercises he had performed at the school in Zurich, Frutiger came up with Univers (1954–57), the first sans serif for photocomposition: an epoch-making font (like Paul Renner's Futura) in its forms and in the unprecedentedly systematic approach to its design, with twenty-one coordinated variants that have proved extraordinarily enduring. It is no accident that Frutiger has produced a refined digital updating of the character, with fifty-nine variants, for Linotype, available since 1997.

Synoptic table of the *Univers* typeface; at the center *Univers 55*, the "standard" face, on the horizontal axes the condensations, on the vertical ones the weights. The odd numbers indicate roman, the even ones italic.

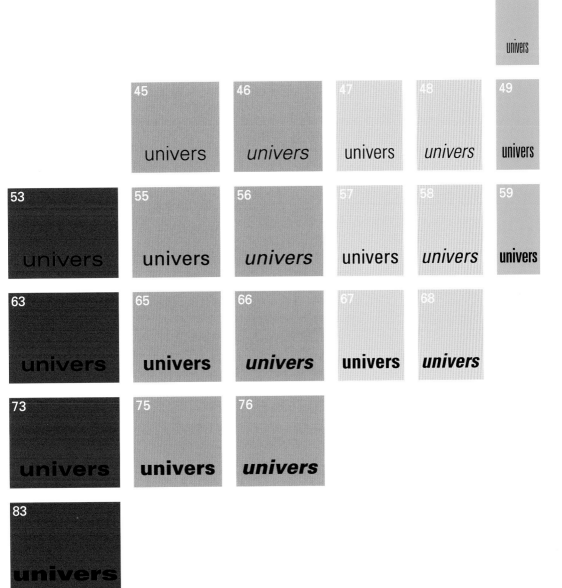

Almost unknown in his own country, and in general familiar only to a few connoisseurs, the work of Aldo Novarese constitutes an extraordinary contribution of Italian ingenuity to that realm of strict aesthetic rigor that is the design of lettering, the tracing of the forms of the alphabet, the invention of typefaces. An art hitherto reserved for the few, which is now experiencing an impetuous and enthusiastic but also confused and often amateurish renaissance in other areas of the world, and the English-speaking countries in particular. Italy, for its part, can boast a historical tradition of capital importance in the art of printing—is the reminder really necessary?—of which all that remains is a gigantic admonitory glow, in the night of the present. Think of another great Aldo, of the importance of the press of Aldus Manutius in Humanistic culture, or the work of Giambattista Bodoni, destined to have a universal influence, to mention just two episodes known to all (just as the names of Raffaello Bertieri and Giovanni Mardersteig will certainly be familiar to students of the arts of the 20th century). But we would also like to treat this discussion of Novarese as an opportunity to reflect on the state of the art of one of the fundamental gifts of Western civilization: the design of the letters of the alphabet. And in effect, looking closely at the dialectic between concrete technical instruments and the abstract means of design, we have to note that, paradoxically, it has taken little more than a decade to make Novarese (a man with a refined understanding and rare experience of the modern applied aesthetics of lettering) at once a sort of survivor from the age of primitive technology and a precious custodian of those "secrets of the art" that run the risk of disappearing in the current situation of apocalyptic fission of centuries of typographic tradition, the result of swift and sweeping, though ultimately predictable, changes in the methods of production.

Aldo Novarese was born in 1920 at Pontestura, a village in the Monferrato. His father, an excise officer, worked in Turin, and moved there with the family. In the Piedmontese capital, Novarese studied first at the Scuola Artieri Stampatori, a training college specializing in printing, where he learned various artistic techniques, largely through the teaching of Francesco Menyey, an instructor of Hungarian origin. He then pursued his interests further at the Scuola di Tipografia G.B. Paravia, where he was to return after the war to teach typographic aesthetics. In 1936, at the age of sixteen, he was taken on at the Studio Artistico of the Fonderia Nebiolo (long directed by Alessandro Butti), where he spent almost forty years of his creative life. Since the 19th century, Nebiolo of Turin had been the main type foundry in Italy (and the only one with an international reputation), but it no longer operates in the sector. In 1938 Novarese won a gold medal at the Ludi Juveniles of the Fascist regime. Drafted shortly after, he was imprisoned for protesting against the outbreak of war and, condemned to a long sentence, was saved by that medal. With the armistice of 1943, he joined the Garibaldi brigade in the resistance to the Nazi-Fascists and lived

A biographical sketch

through a series of atrocious events, which left a deep mark on him. It was sheet luck that he escaped a firing squad. Returning to the Nebiolo foundry after the war, Novarese became director of its art studio in the fifties, taking over from Butti. While engaged in a busy professional practice as a graphic artist of great talent, he took an active part in contemporary cultural life, often in solitary and polemical dispute with his colleagues in Milan. He taught at the school and wrote for the specialist periodicals on the need to promote a true culture of typographic design (and in the very limited range of literature published in Italian in this sector in the second half of the 20th century, his two educational books remain fundamental: *alfa-beta. Lo Studio e il Disegno del Carattere* of 1964 and *Il Segno Alfabetico* of 1971). But he also investigated on his own initiative the illustrious traces of the history of writing and printing (by studying the masterpieces preserved in the Libreria Marciana, for instance) which are so extraordinarily abundant in this country and yet so neglected. He also tried his hand at painting and photography, with more than satisfying results. In this climate of general creativity, Aldo took part from the outset in the now famous Rencontres that were held in Haute-Provence, where in 1957 he presented his system for classifying typefaces, which was widely adopted and appreciated.

In 1975, after four decades of work, Novarese was obliged with great sadness to leave Nebiolo. Forced to restructure, it closed down its typographic department, print foundry and art studio, wiping out a long and honored heritage of ideas, achievements and equipment. From the second half of the seventies, Novarese took on a new lease of life, working as a retiring and masterly designer of letters.

Novarese's fonts

In quantitative terms alone, Novarese's contribution to contemporary typographic design has been extraordinary: more than one hundred typefaces, consisting of a total of about three hundred series of different "weights" (and we are not talking about sketches, studies or ideas, but complete sets of characters, present—many of them to this day—in the catalogues of the best international foundries). The impressive chronological sequence of around thirty fonts (in about one hundred series) that Novarese designed for Nebiolo between the forties and seventies, and over seventy (in more than two hundred series) that he has produced since the mid-seventies speaks for itself. But it would also be of great value to illustrate and examine them analytically, so they can be comparatively assessed.

Novarese's work at Nebiolo commenced, and continued for a long time, under the direction of Alessandro Butti, a figure of considerable importance in the field of typeface design in Italy. In the second half of the thirties, Nebiolo had presented at least three fonts that are of interest, for different reasons: in 1935, Da Milano's Neon, still unique of its kind; in 1937, Brünnel's Resolut; and in 1939, Butti's Landi Echo, an exquisite conceptual variation of the Welt typeface. And in fact a further variation of Welt was one of Novarese's first

previous pages: *Nebiolo*, cover of promotional leaflet, 1967; the photograph shows the hands of Aldo Novarese (Pontestura 1920, Turin 1995) and some of the typefaces that he helped to design.

above: *Nebiolo*, cover of promotional leaflet, n.d.; initials of some typefaces designed by Aldo Novarese: from the top, *Cigno*, 1954, *Egizio*, 1953 on, *Microgramma*, 1952 on, *Normandia*, 1946 on, *Fontanesi*, 1951, *Augustea*, 1951.

una grande famiglia di caratteri lineari della Società Nebiolo Torino

Recta

Recta, cover of the specimen
book, 1958; this was one
of the first "Italian responses"
to the sans serif typefaces
of the Swiss school.

160

typefaces, Landi Linear (1943). In the forties, Novarese followed up the twin Etruria fonts (1940–42) and Express (1940–43) with the Normandia family (1946–49 with Butti, and 1952) and Iniziali Athenaeum (1947). The fifties opened with the ironic rococo of Fontanesi (1951–54) and the uninhibited anachronism of the lowercases of Nova Augustea; at the same time, the highly successful Egizio fonts (1953–57) were accompanied by three scripts: Cigno (1954), Juliet (1954–55) and Ritmo (1955). In the second half of the fifties, the refined classical spirit of the Garaldus family (from 1956) had its modern counterpart in the Recta font, the "Italian response" to the flood of Swiss sans serifs in the second half of the 20th century (notably Miedinger's Helvetica and Frutiger's Univers).

Then, at the beginning of the sixties, after Estro (1961) and Exempla (1961), Eurostile (1961–62), which attracted so much foolish controversy, attained the lofty goal of embodying the "spirit of the time" in a typeface, while the contemporary Patrizia, still unexploited commercially, demonstrated Novarese's intuitive capacities. Just after the middle of the sixties, Novarese attempted to repeat the double move (Garaldus/Recta) that he had carried out successfully ten years earlier, with two other typefaces: Magister (1966) and Forma (1966). At the same time his sensitivity in the interpretation of history was demonstrated by Oscar (1966). After the unashamed clone of Lambert's Compacta represented by Metropol (1967), Elite confirmed that Novarese was at his ease with modern scripts. Designed at the beginning of the seventies, the Fenice series represented a true renaissance. And even if the story of Nebiolo was about to come to an end, the fonts that Novarese designed shortly before he left are interesting.

Stop (1971) hit the bull's eye in the quest for a logographic character, achieving a planetwide success that shows no sign of diminishing. The Egyptian typeface Dattilo (1974), the last to be created for Nebiolo, brought forty years of dedication to a close with the sarcastic flavor of the typewriter character. In the mid-seventies, Novarese embarked on a new period of creativity: as a freelance "letter artist," he has designed dozens of fonts since that time, many of them initially for manufacturers of transfers. It is impossible here, for reasons of space, to give a full account of the last twenty years. So we will confine ourselves to three fonts, among the most important of the period: Mixage (1977), an elegant sans serif for Haas; Symbol (1982), another notable sans serif for ITC; and, from shortly before, the typeface that has made his name known to all those who design and work with lettering, a masterpiece of typographic design of the seventies, the series of transitional fonts for ITC entitled Novarese (1978).

There is one thing that needs to be borne in mind. The historical repertory of typefaces that we have inherited today has grown over the centuries as a means of "artificial writing," in a de facto technologically stable environment—the "Gutenberg workshop"—by accumulating the sophisticated know-how of generations of engravers of punches as

Ars est celare artem

well as by sifting selective and adaptive responses to the changing needs of society. For centuries the assimilation and mastery, through copying, of this heritage was the only means of training, and is probably still fundamental. "Lettering is a precise art and strictly subject to tradition," wrote Arthur Eric Rowton Gill, expressing an opinion that we would like to able to subscribe to today. "The New Art notion, that you can make letters of whatever shape you like, is as foolish as the notion that you can make houses any shape you like. You can't, unless you live all by yourself on a desert island."

So in the industrial arts we are dealing with here it seems that innovation can hardly mean unorthodox, unprecedented, incessant novelties, acceptable on desert islands: the "new" as pure difference, as continual diversity, as inexhaustible epiphany, is only a cliché, devoid of meaning, fruit of the ideology of merchandise and the market. From our perspective, innovation should be seen as any change capable of linking in the most appropriate way the history of adaptation embodied in any artifact to changes in the means/instruments of production, whatever they may be. This entails an adjustment, a coherent modification, of the conceptual and ideational instruments, which have always been slower to change than machines, being caught between the flow of common ways of thinking and random individual events. The challenge of the present age (of every age?) appears to be to seek answers to its questions in the past: finding mental approaches appropriate to the new means, modifying ideas without losing collective memories. Only by seeking to discover the mutations of the artifact implied by and consistent with the change in the means/instruments is it possible to liberate our creative potential. This is precisely the kind of problem that designers of letters find themselves facing again today.

In the second half of the 20th century the instruments and the means by which "pages" (and letters) are made visible and therefore prepared for printing have already undergone two radical changes. At ever increasing speed, since the time of the Linotype and Monotype typesetting machines, the first great typographic revolution since Gutenberg, since the sixties the postwar publishing industry has seen units dedicated to photocomposition predominate in the preprinting sector, reducing the preparation of plates to a purely technical performance. Then, in the eighties, there was the breakthrough of computer-based DTP systems that have essentially turned photocomposition units into mere output devices. Thus a process of progressive, entropic "cooling by expansion" has led from "hot" composition (by character, word, line) to "cold" composition (by column) and to today's "virtual" composition (by page). In very brief outline (with all the approximations that this entails), we can say that type, in its very long, primitive phase, was three-dimensional and heavy; in its second phase, the character became practically two-dimensional and almost weightless; today, letters are simply the emission of light.

In this way, seen theoretically, the very foundations of the design of type have been undermined. Historically, the shapes of the letters of

Nebiolo, cover of promotional leaflet for the English-speaking market, n.d.
Nova Augustea, cover of the specimen book, n.d.; the *Nova Augustea* typeface (1951) completed the series of uppercases of the *Augustea*, derived from the Latin lapidary capital, with lowercase letters: it was, therefore, a typeface completely "invented" by Aldo Novarese.
Egizio, cover of the specimen book, n.d.

nova Augustea

L'alfabeto maiuscolo latino raggiunse la perfezione di forma nel periodo Augusteo; il minuscolo, nel periodo rinascimentale. Il primo proviene dai segni greci e fenici; il secondo, dalle scritture umanistiche e carolingie. Accordare questi due stili in un unico carattere fu una difficile impresa dei prototipografi che operarono in Italia, i quali lo adottarono e lo impressero con successo nei loro torchi; ma non tutti riuscirono nel loro intento. Creare un minuscolo pari per bellezza al classico maiuscolo romano, è il tema che la Società Nebiolo si è posta al fine di completare la già famosa serie Augustea, ispirata alle purissime forme del lapidario. Alla Nova Augustea tonda, qui presentata, seguirà la serie corsiva, in corso di studio.

Eurostile

CRÉATION DE LA SOCIETÀ NEBIOLO TORINO

Eurostile, cover of the specimen
book, 1962; this typeface was
an evolution of Microgramma,
designed for use in very small
bodies by Alessandro Butti
and Aldo Novarese in 1952.

our "artificial writing" constitute a hypertrophied branch of the tree of "natural writing" in Western civilization. Natural writing in itself requires flexible copies of the models of letters and implies actual connections between the letters to form words, with a tendency to reinforce mutual visual relations. Artificial writing, on the other hand, involves rigid copies of the models of letters, with a purely perceptual link between them which forms the basis of their visual unification into words, by proximity. In other words, calli-graphy (natural writing par excellence) is based on the continuity of the lines traced, reflecting a certain figurative arrangement. But typo-graphy (i.e. artificial writing, since the time of Gutenberg) is founded on the objective separation of the impression made by the punch, which demonstrates the essentially monogrammatic nature of the artifact we call "type."

The Copernican revolution of virtual writing today represents a challenge and calls everything into question. This is true not just of the astonishing current trend towards perfection in the digital forms of characters (by exploiting the power of mathematical, vectorial descriptions), which may permit the full recovery of the "wisdom of the ancients," for example in the optical adjustments made to the variations of bodies; there is also the hope that it will be possible to put an end to the now quite unjustified (except for historical reasons) nightmare of the different units of measurement used in typography, which are not metric and are incompatible, even to common sense.

There is more: virtual writing permits, or at least suggests a rethinking of the forms of our typographic alphabet (should it still be called type?), of the appearance of printed letters. As the separation of letters is no longer intrinsically necessary, their design does not have to be governed exclusively by a monogrammatic principle. On the contrary, it is legitimate (at the very least) to envisage a new hybridization, whether polygrammatic or even mildly figurative. It is time to give serious consideration to the fact that today, after centuries (and with extremely powerful instruments of design and control), designers of letters can once again be "masters" of their artifacts and their means of production: as with the early Humanist typographers, are the innovative efforts of digital typographers set to play an active part in a new Renaissance? The rigorous approach that Aldo Novarese has quietly and stubbornly continued to adopt, in the teeth of the brash and mundane vulgarity of today's graphic designers and artists, underlines the need for ethical choice in a time of confused self-gratification and inane calls to order. It encourages us to stress an important conviction: a strict discipline of design can still serve to test and verify, by means of concrete (hence always different) results, the appropriateness of the industrial arts in their response to lasting needs deeply rooted in the human soul, needs that are individual as well as collective, objective and communicative as well as subjective and aesthetic, without the narcissism and self-indulgence typical of today's show business and marketing wars.

below: *Stop*, cover
of the specimen book, 1971;
a typeface still popular all over
the world today (p. 203).
right: *Nebiolo*, cover
of promotional leaflet for
the Spanish-speaking market,
n.d.

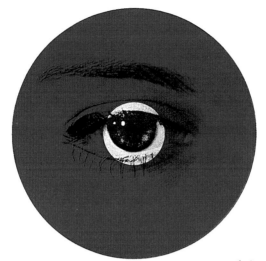

Caleidoscopio de tipos **Nebiolo**

giovanni pintori   effect of synthesis

"His best work as a painter, graphic artist and designer is the effect of synthesis." So Libero Bigiaretti wrote of Giovanni Pintori in 1967 (in one of the *Quaderni di Imago* published by Bassoli), grasping the essence of his achievement. The quality Bigiaretti refers to was a singular capacity for iconic simplicity, a distinctive gift for the production of concentrated and pulsating visual energies, a magical ability to extract, direct and reduce representation to an idea of vibrant essence, through a mysterious alliance between mind and hand.

These gifts enabled this extraordinary Italian visual designer to respond (in a manner at once stringent and imaginative) to the requirements of Olivetti's coordinated advertising image over a very long stretch of the 20th century. But let us take things in order. Wiry, olive-complexioned, rather below average height, with a very prickly character: this is how reporters described Giovanni Pintori, known to everyone simply as Pintori, born at Tresnuraghes, in the province of Nuoro (Sardinia), in 1912.

In 1930, at the age of eighteen, Pintori won a scholarship to the ISIA (Istituto Superiore per Industrie Grafiche) in Monza, where he studied until 1936, under teachers of the caliber of Marcello Nizzoli, Giuseppe Pagano and Edoardo Persico—three of leading exponents of the original rationalist research carried out in Italy between the wars and prominent figures in the country's artistic and architectural culture.

Pintori went on to collaborate on the design of both the exhibition of graphic art at the 7th Milan Triennale and the famous exhibition of Italian aeronautics held in 1934, again at the Triennale's Palazzo dell'Arte in Milan.

In 1937 Adriano Olivetti hired him to work in his company's publicity department: a role whose implications Pintori explored for over thirty years, becoming its artistic director in 1950 and earning a justly lasting international reputation. In fact Pintori left an indelible mark on the business communication of the Italian company most attentive to what journalists now call the "design effect," to the point where a colossus such as IBM also felt the need for a structured corporate identity, a task which it then placed in the able hands of Paul Rand.

So Olivetti was a memorable and exemplary case in the history of industrial design, comparable to the prototypical German experience of AEG with Peter Behrens: notwithstanding the years that have passed, therefore, the documentation assembled in the volume *Design Process Olivetti 1908–1983*, published by Comunità, remains fundamental.

During the rest of his career, after opening a studio of his own in 1968, Pintori was to devote himself (with some diffidence) mainly to painting. (The same happened to another great and not much older visual designer whom it is worth placing alongside him, for the affinities in their visual work, in an imaginary gallery of the protagonists

left: Giovanni Pintori (Tresnuraghes 1912, Milan 1999), in a photograph by Ugo Mulas, c. 1965. below: *Olivetti 84*, detail of an advertisement, n.d.; Giovanni Pintori belonged to the group of graphic artists—Marcello Dudovich, Xanti Schawinsky, Herbert Bayer, Marcello Nizzoli, Costantino Nivola, Erberto Carboni, Max Huber, Egidio Bonfante, Raymond Savignac, Walter Ballmer, Franco Bassi, Jean-Michel Folon, Perry King, Jean Raymond, Milton Glaser, Alan Fletcher and Enzo Mari—that since the thirties helped to make the Olivetti image synonymous with "graphic excellence," with a particular interaction between two- and three-dimensional design.

of Italian 20th-century graphics, the architect Franco Grignani.) An intransigent designer, Pintori worked on a series of memorable campaigns for Olivetti products with great thoroughness in his three decades of imaginative activity in the advertising department. It is hard to pick out just one example: they covered the launch of the Studio 42 and Studio 44 typewriters in 1937–39 (when he worked alongside the outstanding designer Leonardo Sinisgalli), the Lexicon in 1953, the Lettera 22 in 1954–55, Tetractys in 1956, the Divisumma in 1956–57, the Electrosumma, also in 1956–57, and the Raphael, in 1961.

Also noteworthy was his design of the Olivetti showroom in Milan in 1963 and various typefaces for typewriters in the late fifties. Then there was a celebrated cover for *Fortune*, in March 1953, when his reputation crossed the Atlantic with an exhibition at the MoMA in New York. The show eventually traveled to London and Paris and ended up at the Venice Biennale—one of the many tributes, awards and exhibitions that marked Pintori's career.

The unique synthesis that Olivetti represented in the world of (multinational) corporations, through its combination of a vast range of entrepreneurial, manufacturing, organizational, creative and above all cultural skills (it was a true engine of the Italian economy) was fully matched by the distinctive visual synthesis of Pintori's fascinating printed work. It is highly personal as well as typically Italian, with a striking lyrical rationalism that quite clearly reveals the continuity of the expressive research conducted by many artists in this country from the late thirties to the end of the fifties.

In an age like the present, inexorably globalized and standardized, it would be interesting to consider whether Pintori's specific qualities, his universally recognized and starkly effective mode of expression, do not have their roots deep in a tradition that enabled them to develop in an original way: the indigenous, autochthonous history of the graphic arts in Italy which, before being necessarily betrayed by anyone who intends to practice them, still needs—in my view—to be understood, explored and handed on.

Olivetti from the Manuscript to the Electroscript and *Olivetti Tiredness is Not a Virtue*, advertisements, 1963. *Olivetti Lexicon*, detail of poster, 1953.

Il Landgravio di Assia,
nel Seicento, aveva un consigliere,
di nome Orphyreus.
Costui aveva elaborato una ruota
a compartimenti radiali:
in ognuno era chiusa una sfera.
Girando la ruota, le sfere
avrebbero dovuto
spostare di continuo
il centro di gravità.
E così la ruota
non si sarebbe fermata mai più.
Ma è solo vero moto perpetuo
è quello della ricerca scientifica
e del progresso tecnico.

Il solo vero moto perpetuo
è quello della ricerca scientifica
e del progresso tecnico.
La Olivetti ne è un esempio.

Dal manoscritto all' elettroscritto

Chi ha attrezzato i suoi uffici
con le Elettriche Olivetti
ha anticipato il progresso
ed è nella giusta direzione.
Nei paesi che hanno
il più alto livello di vita
si comprano oggi
tante macchine per scrivere
elettriche quante a mano.
Molte delle lettere che il vostro ufficio
ha ricevuto oggi
sono state scritte ieri
su di una elettrica Olivetti;
scriverà una Elettrica Olivetti domani
le lettere che firmerete voi.

olivetti
scrittura elettrica

Villard de Honnecourt,
architetto francese del secolo XIII,
era giunto alla conclusione
che un certo numero di pesi mobili
disposti lungo la circonferenza d'una ruota
avrebbe determinato,
con un perpetuo squilibrio,
un moto perpetuo.
Il disegno che Villard ci ha lasciato
è uno dei tanti illusioni
d'un moto senza motore e senza fatica.
Solo l'elettricità ha consentito
di introdurre ovunque il motore
e di diminuire dovunque la fatica.

Solo l'elettricità
ha consentito
di introdurre
ovunque il motore:
anche nelle macchine per scrivere.

La stanchezza non è una virtù

Finisce sotto i nostri occhi
l'età della dattilografa
che pesta sui tasti.
Nelle Elettriche Olivetti
c'è un motore che ruota:
costante, silenzioso, veloce.
basta sfiorare i tasti
e l'energia del motore
imprime i caratteri.
L'alfabeto vi fila via dalle dita.
L'elettroscrittura è la forma moderna
della dattilografia.

olivetti
scrittura elettrica

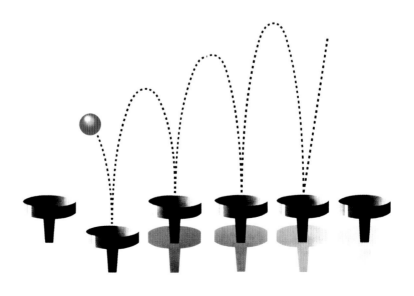

above: *Olivetti What an Electric Page is Worth* and *Olivetti Another Way of Writing*, advertisements, 1963.
right: *Olivetti 10 Factories*, advertisement, n.d.

10 fabbriche Olivetti:
eguali metodi, macchine eguali.

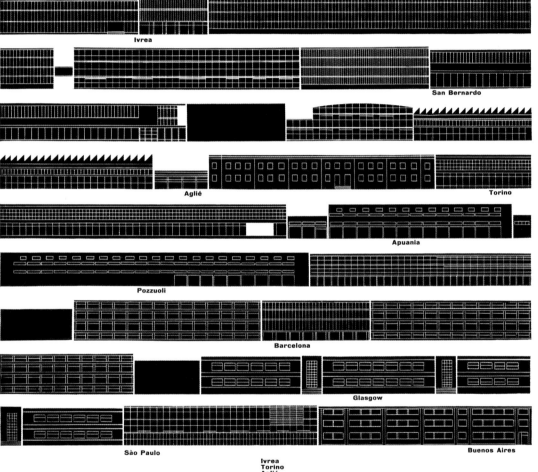

Ivrea

San Bernardo

Aglié

Torino

Apuania

Pozzuoli

Barcelona

Glasgow

Sào Paulo

Buenos Aires

Ivrea
Torino
Aglié
San Bernardo
Apuania
Pozzuoli
Barcellona
Glasgow
Buenos Aires
Sào Paulo

In questi stabilimenti si produce secondo un piano comune di lavoro unitario. I metodi costruttivi sono quelli più progrediti dell'odierna meccanica di precisione; le fabbriche Olivetti dei due continenti promuovono e si scambiano esperienze preziose. I materiali impiegati, i collaudi e i controlli, i criteri per la selezione del personale, sono, in ogni stabilimento, identici. Anche l'assistenza ai clienti, ha in ogni paese del mondo i medesimi caratteri di tempestività ed esattezza. Ovunque si scriva e si calcoli, riconoscibili principi di organizzazione industriale e di stile commerciale si associano al nome della Olivetti.

olivetti

previous page: note at bottom
the Olivetti trademark, designed
by Marcello Nizzoli in 1956
and which signified, according
to its author, "beginning without
end."
above: *Olivetti 82 Diaspron*,
detail of the poster, 1959.
right: *Olivetti Graphika*,
advertisement, 1958.

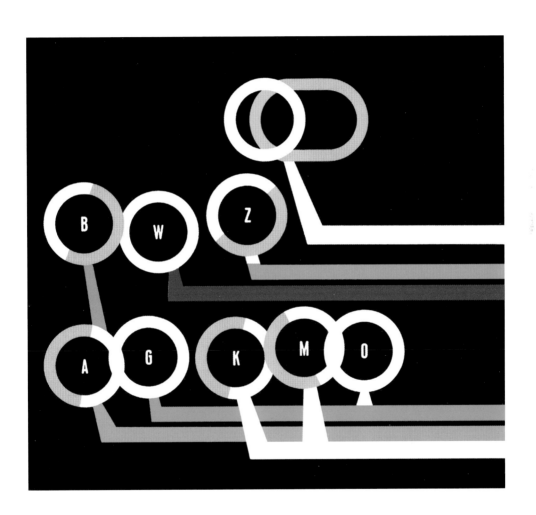

I vantaggi della contabilità meccanizzata sono
oggi essenziali anche per la piccola azienda,
che deve puntare sulla tempestività delle for-
niture, dei pagamenti e degli incassi. Sul piano
dell'attrezzatura produttiva, certi utensili sono
riconosciuti indispensabili tanto al grande stabilimento che all'officina semiartigianale. È lo
stesso, ai fini di un efficiente amministrazione,
vale per la macchina contabile: anche la piccola
industria con quindici o venti operai o l'ufficio
commerciale organizzato su poche decine di
movimenti giornalieri non possono più affidarsi
per la loro contabilità ai sistemi tradizionali.
Persistere nella contabilità manuale è un lusso
antieconomico.

olivetti MACCHINE CONTABILI

Anche la macchina contabile è Olivetti. Accanto
alle macchine per scrivere e alle calcolatrici,
in migliaia di grandi e piccole industrie, di grandi
e piccoli uffici commerciali, in tutti i paesi del
mondo, macchine contabili Olivetti portano quo-
tidianamente il contributo della loro efficienza
e i concreti vantaggi della meccanizzazione.
Anche senza alcuna esperienza di contabilità
meccanica, qualsiasi impiegato è in grado di
servirsi nel giro di poche ore delle macchine
contabili Olivetti.

olivetti MACCHINE CONTABILI

Per la piccola fabbrica, con un magazzino e
un amministrazione da tenere in ordine; per
l'ufficio vendite che deve controllare scadenze
periodiche di effetti e di pagamenti dilazionati;
per il grossista che deve conoscere in ogni
momento la disponibilità delle varie merci e la
situazione contabile di ogni cliente; per il bilan-
cio della piccola amministrazione comunale;
per regolare gli approvvigionamenti dell'albergo;
per l'economato della comunità; per l'ammini-
stratore di stabili e condomini che ha bisogno
di seguire continuamente la posizione degli in-
quilini e la rateazione delle spese: macchine
contabili Olivetti.

olivetti MACCHINE CONTABILI

Olivetti Accounting Machines,
advertisements, 1963; in these
ads—in which the letters that
make up the name Olivetti are
taken apart and reassembled
into totems—the extent
to which Giovanni Pintori was
influenced by contemporary
research in painting is evident.
Giovanni Pintori also designed
the *Olivetti* logotype that,
based on an original design
by Camillo Olivetti, has been
revised several times over the
course of time, by designers
like Xanti Schawinsky, Marcello
Nizzoli and Walter Ballmer (who
produced the present version
in 1970).

ßßfranco grignani gestaltung

A solitary and rigorous master, a refined and methodical seeker after the "truth" of visual form, the visible word and the eloquent image, painter and photographer (you see the kind of vocabulary I'm going to use, at the risk of a putdown from distinguished academics!): this was the artist and architect Franco Grignani. Born at Pieve Porto Morone (Pavia) in 1908, he died in early 1999 in silence, passing away after prolonged suffering supported with great dignity. Grignani trained in the art of design at the Turin Polytechnic (1929–33) in the halcyon, early days of the indigenous Italian rationalist movement, as sober and somber as it was fertile and dialectical.

Stunned and confused by the series of heavy losses that we have borne recently, I remember him with reverent admiration and dutiful veneration in these lines, written immediately after hearing the fatal news.

After participating, as a painter, in a late but fertile period of Futurism (quite an achievement in such a traditionalist city as Turin), Grignani's development encountered the international avant-garde movements, in particular European abstraction, fostering a deep interest in the psychology of the perception of form. Out of this came, in the fifties, his own dynamic version of Op Art *ante litteram* (I know I'm being anachronistic, so not a good historian, in writing this), years before it gained a name and fame. His full mastery, perfect command and lofty domination of the rules of perception found repeated expression in his visual experiments in virtual movement, optical illusions and evasions, sub-perceptions, distortions, *moirés*, dilations, blurs and so on, applied without pause or respite or break to a formal-expressive universe that out of lazy taxonomic convenience we are accustomed to call painting and graphics (whether in publishing or advertising), through images, patterns, signs and words.

Ever since the thirties Grignani had worked in the field of graphics (architecture of information, we would call it today and Massimo Vignelli would acquiesce), contributing to the corporate communications of firms such as Borletti, Breda Nardi, Cremona Nuova, Dompé, Domus, Mondadori, Montecatini, SPI and the Triennale.

His lasting role as artistic director of the publisher Alfieri & Lacroix was of particular significance, as it produced an extraordinary integration of concise, thoughtful texts (all written by himself) and images: writings made up of images; or rather, text that becomes image and at the same time image that becomes text, anticipating a fusion characteristic of the present day. Universally familiar is his trademark for virgin wool: a paradigmatic example of his approach to the design of a symbol that becomes at once signifier and signified.

He was also, for twenty-six years, art director of *Pubblicità in Italia*, a magazine devoted to visual design for promotional and commercial ends. The author of perceptive essays on the visual arts, Grignani was often asked to give lectures in Europe and the US. We invited

left: Photographic Self-portrait of Franco Grignani (Pieve Porto Morone 1908, Milan 1999), n.d. below: Pure Virgin Wool, international mark of quality, 1964; an aloof but certainly not a marginal figure, Franco Grignani played the leading role in the design of this famous brand.

him to the presentation of the first issue of *Casabella* and saw him
there, standing out amidst the crowd at the back of the room. We
received spontaneous and sincere appreciation, keen and blunt en-
couragement and courteous but firm criticism, as was his gruff way.
We chatted about this and that immediately afterwards: he was
irritated by a slogan that was in circulation, "the end of history"
(ideologies, values, etc.). A rather stupid but effective slogan for
idle journalists and above all intellectuals (dilettante, coherent, in-
coherent, barstool or armchair, take your pick). *Pour épater les
bourgeois et les bourgeoises encore.* It was hardly a coincidence
that the slogan was of Japanese-American origin. It makes a pair
with *The End of Print*, something that astute charlatans of "contemporary graphics" rave about: a widely acclaimed, i.e. ecumeni-
cal, success matched—in my view—by an (unpublished, but real,
relevant and very topical) *Beginning of Reprint*. We remain, however, in our "little old world of the late 20th century, which," as
Mario Tronti has written in some illuminating pages, "should be
looked at with sober eyes, as de facto reality, behind the ideological spectacle of this global and virtual, so-called postmodern. In the
end a return of the 19th century has defeated our own century...
Let us be honest and call this what it is: an age of Restoration. But
without Romanticism. Indeed, essentially neoclassical. An indecently
futuristic neoclassicism."
Pax tibi, Franco. *Nec moriar. "On oi theoì filoùsin apothnéskei néos,"*
to quote Menander. Peace be on you, who *néos* still were, with nine-
ty springs already on those broad shoulders with their elegant bear-
ing and unforgettable deportment, those of a man one naturally
deferred to, because of that aura of authority that surrounded you.

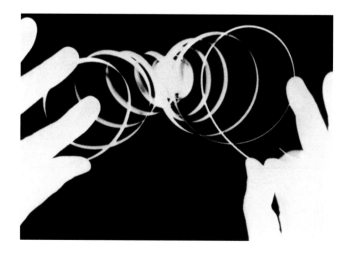

franco grignani

foto grafica

Otto Croy

Editoriale A/Z Milano

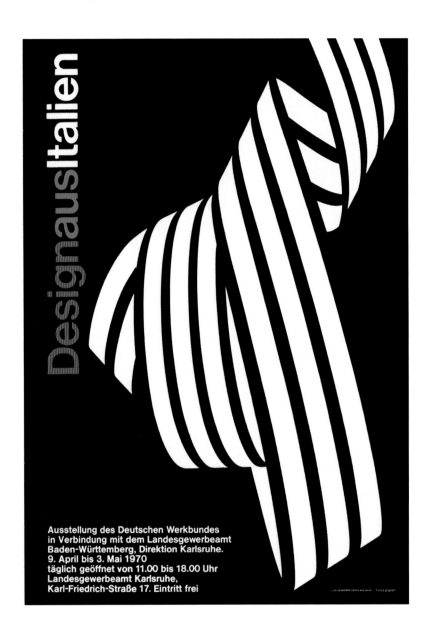

Design from Italy, poster
for the exhibition at Karlsruhe,
1970.

Geometria avvolgente
continua mutevole,
tradotta fisica
nel suo esistere dinamico
e dalla qualità di stampa.
Immagine che esce
da macchine perfette
condotte da nuove tecniche.
Tutti sanno che è
una stampa
della tipolitozincografica
Alfieri e Lacroix.

franco grignani

sd

above and on the three
following pages: *Alfieri
& Lacroix*, advertisements;
seven of the over one hundred
and fifty that Franco Grignani
produced between 1952
and the seventies.

Simbolo delle rotative
dell'inchiostrazione fluida
delle carte calandrate
dei quartini ottavi
sedicesimi
dei controlli elettronici
della velocità
della perfezione

questa è la vostra Alfieri & Lacroix

1960

La materia grafica così libera o duttile, apre le porte a nuove infinite possibilità creative. Sulle superfici corrono i valori tipografici e compositivi, gli stessi che guardati da prospettive diverse ci offrono altre emozioni. La grafica pubblicitaria, sottile, sensibile e inventiva cerca il "nuovo". Lo realizzeremo accanto ad un grande organismo grafico potentemente attrezzato. È l'Alfieri & Lacroix: macchine, maestranze e programmi per i compiti dell'alta grafica.

1960

1960

1961

Alfieri & Lacroix: 27 serie di caratteri tipografici
in chiaro, in nero, nerissimo, filettati, allungati, fiori per il giardino tipografico.

Bodoni
Garamond
Moderno
Africa
Baskerville
Mainperle
Romano inglese
Simbaldi
Antiqua
Nilo
Grotesque
Cantale
Italico allungato
Stilo
Quirino
Landi
Triennale
Futura
Normanno
Inkunabula
Cairoli
Romano allungato
Hastile
Etrusco
Novecento
Pagamini
Normandia

Per Natale e per
il millenovecentosessantuno
scegliete per i vostri clienti
e per i vostri omaggi
regali apprezzati e graditi:
l'almanacco artistico italiano
con cinquantadue
tavole a colori,
pitture di grandi maestri italiani
di ogni tempo,
e il calendario libro d'arte
pubblicazione
di formula originale brevettata.
Prenotateli chiedendo
la cedola di commissione libraria
ad Alfieri & Lacroix
Milano via Mantegna 6

1963

Alfieri & Lacroix adverts are unique in the Italian panorama for at least three reasons: Franco Grignani wrote his own texts, always allusive and never straightforward; they reject the logic of the trademark, i.e. of the fixed and standardized presence of the mark and/or logotype; they are the fruit of a dynamic oscillation between typography and photography, with one or the other prevailing at different times. In 1978, Franco Grignani estimated the number of "experiments" he had carried out in the two intersecting fields at fifteen thousand.

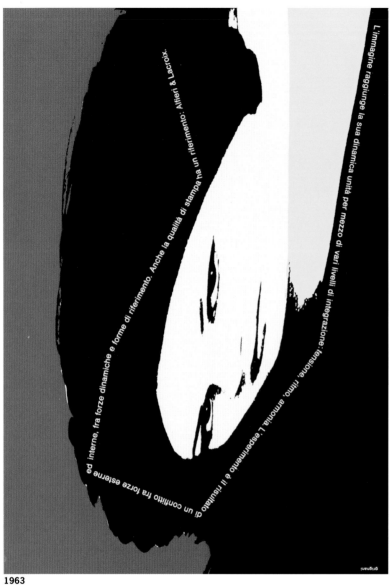

Text on image:

L'immagine raggiunge la sua dinamica unità per mezzo di vari livelli di integrazione: tensione, ritmo, armonia. L'esperimento è il risultato di un conflitto fra forze esterne ed interne, fra forze dinamiche e forme di riferimento. Anche la qualità di stampa ha un riferimento: Alfieri & Lacroix.

grignani

1963

186

right: *Typographica*, cover of issue
no. 16, 1959; the magazine edited
by the Briton Herbert Spencer
(1925–2002) investigated
the multiple aspects of the written
word. This cover is a confirmation
of the fact that Franco Grignani's
work reached beyond national
borders.

In an experimental series called Kwadraatblad ("square notebook") because of its physical (25 × 25 cm) format as well, presumably, as its ideal-theoretical content, the Dutch typo-lithographic company De Jong & Co. of Hilversum published, in 1967, a booklet with a bright red cover, entitled (fittingly, in new letters) "*new alphabet*" in the English version (*nieuw alfabet*, in the indigenous version). If we skip to the colophon, we read, among other things: ©Wim Crouwel (Total Design) Amsterdam. It wasn't the first of these notebooks, however: the series of Kwadraatbladen, known as Quadrat-Prints in English, rich in other significant episodes, had commenced in 1954, on the initiative of a graphic designer highly active in the promotion of visual culture in his own country and outside. This was Pieter Brattinga, who is also the son of the owner of De Jong & Co.

With sober discretion, this ushered in one of the most interesting experiments in letter design of the second half of the 20th century: clusters of long unraveled lines that are entwined with both the life of its designer and the history of modern alphabets and the visible word. "In 1967, with the introduction of the first electronic devices for phototypesetting," Crouwel was to comment in 1988, "I proposed a monoalphabet font in response to the new functional needs. It was a proposal of an essentially theoretical nature, as some of the letters bore no resemblance to the usual ones. The thing attracted a lot of attention but the attempt was fairly futile, in a period in which functionalism, as it was understood in the spirit of the Bauhaus, was under attack and being declared anti-human and out of date."

Born in Groningen, capital of the region of Friesland in the north of the Netherlands, the thirty-nine-year-old Willem "Wim" Crouwel was already one of the most prominent visual designers in the country by 1967, with an international reputation. After finishing his higher education in his native city at the Minerva Academy (1946–49), a school of applied arts with a sound tradition, and his military service (1949–51), which took him away from home for the first time, Crouwel attended the evening course in typography at the IVKNO (1951–52), Instituut voor Kunstnijverheids Onderwijs (Institute for Education in the Industrial Arts, better known later as the Gerrit Rietveld Academy) in Amsterdam. It was in this city that he started work, with an apprenticeship at Enderberg (1952–54), a specialist in the design of stands and exhibitions, which brought him into contact with Swiss graphic designers for the first time. After opening his own studio in Amsterdam (1954–57), he began a period of collaboration with the interior designer Kho Liang Le (1956–60). He then started to work freelance again (1960–63), before founding and co-directing TD Associatie voor Total Design NV (1963–80) with Friso Kramer, Benno Wissing and the brothers Paul and Dick Schwarz. The partnership, perhaps only comparable, in its structure, inspiration and history, to the originally British Pentagram partnership, made him famous worldwide: a pool of professionals committed to the integrated and rational design of

neu
alphabet

a	een	une	eine
possibility	mogelijkheid	possibilité	möglichkeit
for	voor	pour	für
the	de	le	die
new	nieuwe	développement	neue
development	ontwikkeling	nouveau	entwicklung

an
introduction
for
a
programmed
typography

new alphabet, cover, 1967;
it belonged to a series called
Quadrat-Prints, conceived
to promote the typographic firm
De Jong & Co.

communicative and instrumental artifacts that stemmed from a positive vision of intervention in the human environment.

This is neither the time nor the place to recount the extraordinary story of Total Design, which made a deep mark on the international visual scene in the sixties and seventies under the ideological leadership of Crouwel. Its achievements were exemplary in many fields, especially communications for public institutions. Their work has been documented in numerous exhibitions and publications (to which the reader is referred for further information), and is probably familiar to most people. Later, however, Crouwel was also the consultant and spiritual adviser (1980–85) of the Boymans-van Beuningen Museum in Rotterdam, before becoming its director (1985–93) and then returning, indefatigably, to freelance work (since 1994). Moreover, Crouwel has always combined his successful professional career with teaching, initially at the Royal Art Academy in Den Bosch (1954–57), then at the IVKNO in Amsterdam (until 1963) and finally at the Technical University in Delft (1965–85) and the Royal College of Art in London (1981–85).

So the experiment with the "new alphabet"came at a watershed in Crouwel's career. Perhaps his approach to design could best be described by comparing it with two of the principal exponents of postwar design in the US (a country that has long had many parallels with the Netherlands), as a sort of hybrid between the astute corporate design of Paul Rand (in a more cordial and collective vision of the work) and the effervescent exhibition and communications activity of the Eames husband-and-wife team (tempered by a rational attitude, little inclined to emotivity, and veined with a European taste).

In fact, while continually dealing with letters and the alphabet in his work as a visual designer, Crouwel is not (and has never considered himself to be) a designer of letters, of typefaces. Rather he is an experimenter, on an occasional basis, in appropriate forms for the visual word.

The presentation of the "new alphabet" in the pages of the Quadrat-Print makes clear from the start, in the subtitles on the cover, that it is "a possibility for the new development," i.e. "an introduction for a programmed typography."

What did Crouwel mean by this? The statement he makes further on is explicit: the "new alphabet" is a suggested "new typeface that is better suited than more traditional ones to systems of composition with cathode-ray tubes." In other words, argues Crouwel: "The machine has to be accepted as an essential given, if we want to meet the needs of our time. The amount of information that has to be printed every day, necessarily, has grown to such a point that mechanization is indispensable... But letters have never evolved with machines. The proposed unconventional alphabet shown here is intended merely as an initial step in a direction which could possibly be followed for further research. The means of production that is taken as a starting point is the cathode ray, which corresponds to the same principle as television."

Crouwel believes that a mature machine-based civilization, an age of media and electronics, with the conquest of new spaces, on a micro- and macro-scale (to which the images that illustrate the booklet allude) should be matched at least experimentally by the design of "cathodic" letters, based on the new physical support (the TV monitor) and on the increased flow of information demanded by modern times. Significantly, in the background of this hypothesis, three chains of reasoning are entwined: a precocious awareness of the radical changes under way in systems of textual display (the perfecting of phototype-setting then in course was about to destroy the centuries-old, leaden and immovable essence of Gutenberg's print shop); the urgent need for more rapid production, founded on the sole active variable ("only the speed of manufacture has changed," declares Crouwel in the presentation); the aspiration to control design, or rather a new approach to it, capable of being translated into an exact, rational planning of the design of letters, rooted in mathematics and computing, echoing a theme common in contemporary experimentation, that of the "programmed arts," founded on a theory of construction and exploitation of aesthetic activities that is both impersonal-procedural and logical-abstract.

In this framework, Crouwel formulated the structure of his alphabet. It is a two-dimensional grid of 5×9 units, in which each letter and its relative variations of weight and color (from "light" to "black," from "condensed" to "expanded," as well as "slanted," to use the classical terminology of typefaces) are identified by means of an associated code of five variables: a/b/c/d/x. Of these a is the number of vertical units (odd), b the lines per vertical unit (200 per cm), c the horizontal units (odd, minimum: face of the letter + 4), d the lines per horizontal unit (200 per cm) and x the units of the face of the letter (odd). It is obvious that the possible variations, through combination of the individual parameters, once the strokes of the single letters have been defined, are innumerable as well as easily "programmable," by analogy of variables, to obtain particular effects. The whole thing appears to be, in conclusion, a scientific-mathematical procedure made up of one-to-one operations, of controlled variables, that makes it possible to describe and configure a new alphabet, the logical outcome of clear premises.

So far, in our examination of the "new alphabet" we have simply followed the programmatic declarations of its designer. But ought we really trust and openly rely on the author's intentions, on his own descriptions of the design, or are there other elements at stake, concealed beneath so much avowed rationality?

It would be worth verifying the degree to which these statements correspond to the actual artifact presented in the Quadrat-Print. To give a coherent response, we need to take another look at the booklet, examining the figures closely. And at once we find, even on the cover, not one but two alphabets: one (positive, black on white) made up of solid orthogonal lines, fine rectangles whose articulations are formed by joints at 45 degrees or, more precisely, by the filling of half a square unit of the module along the diagonal, so that the joint is in fact an isosceles triangle with right-angled sides equal to 1 and a hypotenuse equal to the square root of 2; the other alphabet (negative, white spots on black) is made up of a series of dots (one per unit of the module), where the junctions are simply the dots set at the points of articulation.

So what do the two alphabets have in common, apart from the obvious but misleading reference to the basic forms of the electronic signaling devices of the time rather than to the pixels of cathode-ray tubes or the pins of dot-matrix printers? Once the logic of the 5×9 grid has been fixed, what connects the alphabets is, in effect, a sensitive if arbitrary choice of *ur-formen*, original shapes for the entire set of the alphabet (letters, numerals, punctuation marks), simplified as much as they can be without losing their recognizability, in a process that is not new but, on the contrary, has recurred repeatedly in the history of the design of letters—but we will have to come back to this aspect soon. In any case, we can hardly help noticing that, in the specialist literature, the name of "new alphabet" is assigned only to the first, positive set of the two alphabets, suggesting that the critics were rather casual in their reading of the documents.

It also seems worth looking at the whole of Crouwel's output, with a view to finding earlier or even later traces that might help us "place" the invention of the "new alphabet" and the evolution of its use by the author. The published reproductions of sketches and studies for the alphabet (prudently, and quite fairly, dated "circa 1967") reveal, in the first place, a great variety of solutions in progress, sometimes with lower degrees of reduction of the pertinent strokes and various uncertainties, although always anchored to the same concept of minimal material form: a problem—it is well known—common to all the rational-Ulmian designs of the period. Looking back, we quickly find that Crouwel had used exactly the same letters as those of the first of the two alphabets illustrated in the Quadrat-Print in April 1967, for the report and invitation to the congress *Mechanisierung en automatisering in het grafisch bedrijf* staged by the VJGO, an association of young graphic designers, and in September 1966, for the cover of an introductory brochure to the Commission on the Use of Computers, for the fourth congress of the European Federation of Financial Analyst Societies. Which requires us to set back the date of the design of the "new alphabet" by perhaps a couple of years. Going even further back, we come across two very similar covers that are significant for our purposes, Dating from 1960 and 1962 they were designed for the catalogue of the Dutch exhibits at the Venice Biennale. Here the word "Holland" was similarly made up of letters drawn with solid orthogonal strokes and 45-degree joints: an invention that is the direct forerunner of the "new alphabet." In a variant even more sensitive to

The basic form on which the proposed new alphabet is founded.
Each derived letterform has a code number, which is explained in this illustration.

De basis figuur waarop het voorgestelde nieuwe alfabet berust.
Elke afgeleide lettervorm krijgt een codenummer dat in deze figuur wordt verklaard.

La figure basique sur laquelle le nouvel alphabet est reposé.
Chaque forme de lettre dérivée aura un numéro de code, lequel est expliqué dans cette figure.

Basis-Figur, auf der das vorgeschlagene neue Alfabet beruht.
Jeder davon abgeleitete Buchstabe erhähIt eine Codenummer, die in dieser Figur erklärt wird.

Code: a/b/c/d/x

a = variable number of vertical units (odd progression)
b = variable number of lines per vertical unit (200 to the cm)
c = variable number of horizontal units (odd progression, at least: x-height + 4)
d = variable number of lines per horizontal unit (200 to the cm)
x = variable number of units of the x-height (odd progression)

a = variabel aantal verticale eenheden (oneven reeks)
b = variabel aantal lijnen per verticale eenheid (200 per cm)
c = variabel aantal horizontale eenheden (oneven reeks, minstens: x-hoogte + 4)
d = variabel aantal lijnen per horizontale eenheid (200 per cm)
x = variabel aantal eenheden in de x-hoogte (oneven reeks)

a = nombre variable des unités verticales (progression impaire)
b = nombre variable des lignes par unité verticale (200 par cm)
c = nombre variable des unités horizontales (progression impaire, minimum: oeil de la lettre + 4)
d = nombre variable des lignes par unité horizontale (200 par cm)
x = nombre variable des unités dans l'oeil de la lettre (progression impaire)

a = variabele Anzahl vertikaler Einheiten (ungerade Reihe)
b = variabele Anzahl Linien per vertikaler Einheit (200 per cm)
c = variabele Anzahl horizontaler Einheiten (ungerade Reihe, mindestens: x-Höhe + 4)
d = variabele Anzahl Linien per horizontaler Einheit (200 per cm)
x = variabele Anzahl Einheiten innerhalb der x-Höhe (ungerade Reihe)

new alphabet, pp. 8–9.

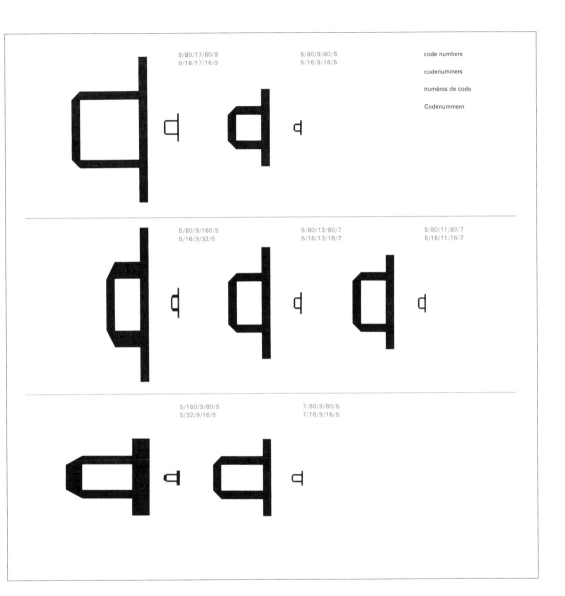

9/80/17/80/9
9/16/17/16/9

5/80/9/80/5
5/16/9/16/5

code numbers

codenummers

numéros de code

Codenummern

5/80/9/160/5
5/16/9/32/5

5/80/13/80/7
5/16/13/16/7

5/80/11/80/7
5/16/11/16/7

5/160/9/80/5
5/32/9/16/5

7/80/9/80/5
7/16/9/16/5

the problem of the junctions, it also appeared on the cover of the catalogue of the Stedelijk Museum dedicated to Brusselmans in 1960 (later reused on the cover of the *Ewald Mataré* catalogue, also published by the Stedelijk Museum in Amsterdam). But its earliest formulation can be recognized in the logo of the headed notepaper for the Rijnja copy center in Amsterdam (circa 1958). All this confirms the idea of a sustained concern with the shapes of letters, continually cropping up in his work. At the beginning of the sixties Crouwel had already found a solution capable of eliminating curves, i.e. geometry of a higher order than straight lines—perhaps because curves were typical of manual, natural writing from the outset, whereas the goal was mechanical lettering, suitable for machines.

Subsequently, though this may appear curious, Crouwel rarely made use of the "new alphabet": indeed he utilized it solely for the cover of the July–August 1968 issue of the Italian periodical *linea grafica*, at the invitation of the far-sighted Franco Grignani, that exceptional and aloof master of Italian visual design. Shortly afterward Crouwel came up with other modular and elementary letters, such as the ones designed in 1968 for the Vormgevers exhibition at the Stedelijk Museum in Amsterdam and for the catalogue of the Erven E. van de Geer print works in the same city; then in 1969 for the "Visuele communicatie Nederland" exhibition, again at the Stedelijk Museum of Amsterdam, in 1970 for the Claes Oldenburg exhibition at the same museum, in 1971 in the alphabet for the Fodor Museum (a well-known set, and a variant of the Vormgevers principle), in 1972 for the pamphlet *Visuele communicatie. Typo Vision International* (another variant of Vormgevers), in 1975 for the calendar of the Erven E. van de Geer print works and in 1976 in the typeface for the Olivetti Politene typewriter and the famous stamps for the Dutch post office (preceded by the 1970 commemorative stamp for Osaka).

And if we trace Crouwel's career in the opposite direction, we find just as many significant experiments with the design of letters, reflecting a lasting and consistent interest in this area of research: the Albersian letters of the Edgar Fernhout poster and the catalogue cover for the Stedelijk van Abbe Museum in Eindhoven in 1963 (whose horizontal cutting recalls the design of the poster for the Dutch exhibit at the 12th Milan Triennale in 1960); the compressed woodcut letters of the Hiroshima poster for the Stedelijk van Abbe Museum in Eindhoven in 1963 (the symptom of a recurrent problem, they reappear, for example, on the cover of the *Robert Muller* catalogue of the Stedelijk Museum of Amsterdam in 1964, and in an orthogonally stiffened version in the headed notepaper for Alice Edeling, in 1969); the vertically split numerals of his personal greeting cards for 1957 (used again in the 1958 greeting cards of the Stedelijk van Abbe Museum in Eindhoven, as well as in the lettering for the cover of the Wessel Couzijn catalogue in 1958). This list does not cover all Crouwel's experiments with the form of letters, but what matters here is not so much the continuity of an experimental attitude, with its highest and most carefully

fodor

thought-out expression in the "new alphabet," as the restricted number of occasions on which he actually made use of it.

Only the widespread revival of interest in the design of typefaces, prompted by the recent emergence of desktop-publishing, has led critics to reexamine the role of the "new alphabet" (and of many other modern alphabets)—culminating in the digital re-edition of Crouwel's four typefaces in 1997, in the Architype series of the British company The Foundry, directed by Freda Sack and David Quay: New Alphabet (in three weights), Stedelijk (Vormgevers, 1968), Fodor (1971) and Gridnik (Politene, 1976).

However, we have not yet answered two questions. Firstly: what is the new alphabet's actual affinity or continuity with other, contemporary "cathodic" fonts? Secondly: where do these austere forms come from and what guarantee does their author offer of their readability and recognizability, clearly designed as they are with the aim of reduction to the essential?

To the first question, we can only say broadly that there is no affinity. The design of alphabets for dot-matrix printers, now rendered obsolete by laser and ink-jet technology, antediluvian on the plane of the form of the letters and now practically abandoned wherever there is a problem of quality, evolved very rapidly as the number of pins in the printhead quickly rose to emulate traditional printed characters. Only in an early phase were the matrices made up of such a small set of dots as to be comparable with the 5×9 units of the "new alphabet"— and even then only in theory, as the uncertain mark produced by the partial overlap of dots certainly had nothing in common with the geometric perfection of lines and diagonals required by the "new alphabet." (In this regard there is an enlightening illustration in the Quadrat-Print: the a of a Garamond typeface and the a of the "new alphabet" are compared, revealing the very high resolution needed to represent them, in a logic of production that is still not vectorial). On the other hand, the fonts dictated by the needs of OCR, the system of optical character recognition being developed at the time, present quite different characteristics: in order to adapt it to OCR techniques, this simplification of the alphabet resulted in a design that was still elaborate in its joins, rich in curves that are strongly reminiscent of the ordinary shapes of both upper and lowercase letters. In short, anything but radical in comparison with the "new alphabet," even though based on minimal matrices, as in the case of the 4×7 grid of the OCR-A (1966), designed to meet the requirements of the US Bureau of Standards, which by 1968 had already been transformed into a matrix of 18×25 for OCR-B, developed under the supervision of Adrian Frutiger on the basis of requests from the European Computer Manufacturers Association since as far back as 1961. Nor can we find affinities with the characters for analogous numerical codes used for banking purposes, such as the very widespread E13B or CMC7, which bear a purely stylistic similarity to the space-flight and robotic tones of a plethora of typefaces that went

6/20/15/20/3
7/24/13/24/7

new alphabet, pp. 12–13
and pp. 14–15.

rapidly out of fashion, such as Colin Brignall's Countdown and the endless related variations in the range of transfers then in use. If anything, the lack of curves, or rather their substitution with 45-degree joints, recalls the design of letters in situations and places where this represented a simplification of execution, as in certain forms of lettering for military aircraft and ships, which were taken up in fonts like Tom Carnase and Renne Bonder's Machine (1970), if it were not for the fact that these are plainly a completely different repertory.

To the second question, relating to the radical choices of minimal serviceable form, we can answer by pointing out (something that has not done been before) that the "new alphabet" is a monoalphabet, i.e. it belongs to that particular family of typefaces that take as their model only one of the two series (historically justified but logically unwarranted) that make up our alphabet: upper and lowercase letters, whose origins can be traced respectively in the Roman lapidary capital (1st century) and the Carolingian minuscule (9th century). Crouwel's alphabet is clearly derived solely from the forms of the minuscule. In addition, if we want to find a more precise historical connection, then we might find it in the half uncial (5th century), with its tetrachord arrangement and the appearance of downstrokes and upstrokes, however contained, as well as the pitchfork shape of the e. Yet the process of tracing pertinent signs is so subtractive in Crouwel, at least for some letters (such as a, g, j, s, x and z), that it suggests adherence to a very strong principle of abstraction rather than a possible mediation in favor of common criteria of recognizability. It is well-known that we read words (groups of letters) as a whole, thanks to their relative isolation (smaller blank spaces between letters than between words)—since our eye runs along the "skyline" of the lines of text, when scanning them during the act of reading—and certainly not by spelling out the letters one by one. It is equally well-known that the recognizability of individual letters (even in groups that form words) is based on their upper half, something that can easily be verified by comparing the two halves (upper and lower) of any letter or group of letters: the upper half contains a greater number of individual strokes, of distinctive elements, of relevant signs, which are what permit rapid mental recognition of the letters. The "new alphabet" ignores this basic principle of perception: the halves of some letters are anything but recognizable and, in many cases (a, f, g, l, p, q, s, x, y and z, apart from the lower doubling bar that artificially identifies m and w), it is necessary to take in their whole shape to distinguish them. In fact some letters have been stripped of significant portions of their usual relevant strokes—the loop of the a, the stem of the f, the lower hooks of the g and the j, the upper hook of the s and the lower hook of the z— while the stiffening of the geometry leads to an abnormal design of the k and x. In addition, pairs of letters such as d and g, k and t, s and z and u and v appear ambiguous. In conclusion, the unorthodox design makes it hard to identify much of the alphabet, and in particular

MACHINE

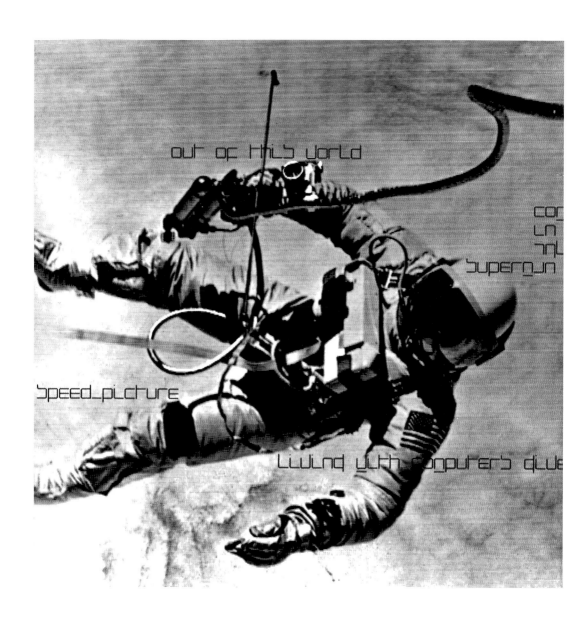

new alphabet, p. 16
and inside back cover.

Example of integrated 'scanned' Typo-graphic.

Voorbeeld van geïntegreerde 'afgetaste' typo-grafiek.

Exemple du typo-graphique 'balayé' et intégré.

Beispiel für eine integrierte 'abgetastete' Typo-Grafik.

above: *Designers*, poster for
the exhibition at the Stedelijk
Museum, 1968; Wim Crouwel
underlined the systematic
intent by emphasizing the grid
on which he constructed
the letters.
bottom right: like the
new alphabet, a preview
of Novarese's *Stop* (p. 166) was
presented by Franco Grignani
in *Linea grafica*.

the letters a, g, j, k, s, x and z. Nor is the situation improved by upper horizontal bar used to indicate capitals.

Minimal material, therefore, does not imply maximum or even normal legibility. If anything, in Crouwel's case it is more a question of respecting an a priori structural norm on which to base the mechanics of the shapes, in a logic of congruence indifferent to the usual criteria of legibility, which naturally require the use of upper and lowercases. The "cathodic" universality of the "new alphabet," therefore, is blatantly contradicted by its scant respect for the historic forms of letters. What was Crouwel's objective, or rather to what other principles did he conform?

To answer this question it is necessary, at this point, to turn to the history of modern lettering, examining a series of 20th-century experiments and recognizing that the themes of both testing of the limits of recognizability of letters and the tendency toward a monoalphabet are not at all new. This will allow us to put Crouwel's "new alphabet" in its rightful place in this continuous process, where it forms a sort of final stage before the subsequent crisis and the radical innovation in the design of typefaces in the digital tempest.

Examples of attempts at a reduction to the minimum form stud the whole history of 20th-century typefaces, as is demonstrated by the cases of A.M. Cassandre's semiomissive Bifur (1929) and, at a distance of forty years, showing just how enduring the problem is, Aldo Novarese's logographic Stop (1970), both founded on the skeleton of capitals with the ambition of identifying the final essence of their form. The ambiguous ideological attraction of a monoalphabet made up of lowercase letters is even stronger, especially in Germany (owing to the frequent use of capital letters in the language), as is apparent from an essay on *The Bauhaus and Typology* written by Laszlo Moholy-Nagy in 1925: "Jakob Grimm had already written all nouns with lowercase initial letters... The celebrated architect Loos argues in his collected essays: 'For Germans, there is a great fracture between written and spoken language. Speaking, we cannot use capital initials. Everyone talks without thinking about uppercase initials. But if a German picks up a pen, he can no longer write as he thinks and talks.' The poet Stefan George and his circle have also made the monoalphabet the basis of their publications. While it can be objected that this is a matter of poetic license, we can add that in 1920, in line with Dr. Porstmann's book *Sprache und Schrift*, even the sober association of German engineers came out in favor of the monoalphabet. It justified this position by arguing that the use of lowercase initials would take nothing away from our writing, but would render it more legible, easier to learn and essentially more economical: there is no point in using twice the number of symbols for a single sound when half will do. These simplifications have practical consequences for the construction of typewriters and for typesetting, and imply a saving on characters and shifts... The Bauhaus has investigated all the problems bound up with typology and has acknowledged the correctness of the arguments adopted in favor of the monoalphabet."

i10
internationale avantgarde 1927-1929
stedelijk museum amsterdam 18-10–18-11 '63

above: *i 10, international avant-garde 1927–1929*, poster for the exhibition at the Stedelijk Museum, 1963; here Jurriaan Schrofer has taken up and perfected the alphabet devised by Josef Albers in 1931 (p. 119).
right: *Bart van der Leck*, poster by Bart van der Leck (Utrecht 1876, Blaricum 1958) for his one-man show at the Voor de Kunst gallery in Utrecht, 1920.

TENTOONSTELLING
v.d. LECK. 12 JAN: 9 FEB:

VOOR DE KUNST
NOBELSTR: UTRECHT

These questions were debated not just at the Bauhaus but in the whole of 20th-century German culture (for a long time, the dominant visual culture in Europe), as is clear from the assumptions of Otl Aicher, for instance, in his famous volume *Typographie* published in 1988. In the meantime, there was an international flowering of experiments in the design of letters. They started with the typefaces of Herbert Bayer—from Universal (1925) to Bayer (1931)—and the monoalphabet of Jan Tschichold (1926–29); then passed through the appeals of Laszlo Moholy-Nagy and the work of Joost Schmidt and Josef Albers at the Bauhaus, the experimental lowercase letters of Paul Renner for the preliminary version of the epoch-making sans serif Futura (1927–30) and mixed systems like those of Kurt Schwitters' Systemschrift (1927) or A.M. Cassandre's peculiar Peignot (1937). Finally they arrived at Max Bill's still immature efforts (1944), the mix of Bradbury Thompson's first Monoalphabet (1945, based on Futura) and later Alphabet26 (1950, based on Baskerville), and culminated in the emblematic attempt in the early sixties, again by Max Bill, to create a "typeface of word-images," that will be "machine-readable, owing to the emphasis on the vowels, and more legible for people: a typeface for our time."

There is no space in this essay to compare and analytically document the variety of these and other experiments along the same lines. I have had to limit myself to listing examples, as part of the scholarly approach essential to any attempt at historical interpretation that goes beyond an uncritical description of its subject. A lot of work still needs to be done, especially in the sparse specialist literature of Italy. Though it is not without significant achievements in the design of alphabets in the 20th century, it is almost oblivious of them, owing to the total lack of studies and a scholarly rather than amateur and extempore interest in the field.

To return to our subject: the case of the "new alphabet" needs to be compared and connected with another tradition, which Crouwel was certainly aware of when he began to reflect on the forms of his alphabet: the indigenous, Dutch tradition of lettering, which had a profound influence on the more radical lines of research in the 20th century. It was practically the promised land of contemporary typography, if only for the extraordinary concentration of type designers at work there.

The Netherlands had a great historical tradition in the art of printing and the design of typefaces, especially in the 16th and 17th centuries: starting, that is, with the French-born Christophe Plantin (1514–89), who made use of the fonts of Guillaume Le Bé, Claude Garamond and Robert Granjon, and the dynasty (active until 1876) founded by his son-in-law Moretus in Catholic Antwerp. Then there was the other eminent family of Elzevir, in Protestant Leyden. In the Dutch "golden age" Christoffel van Dijk (1601–69) was its principal type designer and punchcutter (his characters were in continuous use until 1810). Other prominent punchcutters were Bartholomeus Voskens (†1669) and Nicholas Kis (1650–1702) in Amsterdam.

pagina

above: *Pagina*, masthead of the magazine set in Max Bill's "typeface of word-images," 1964; like Kurt Schwitters (p. 105), he made the outline of the vowels thicker than that of the consonants.

The classical tradition of Dutch lettering was renewed in the first half of the 20th century by such outstanding figures as De Roos and van Krimpen, though they were little known outside the country. Sjoerd Hendrik de Roos (1877–1962), artistic director of the Lettergieterij Amsterdam foundry for thirty years, designed such distinctive typefaces as Hollandse Mediäval (1912), Erasmus Mediäval (1923), Egmont (1933) and De Roos (1947), as well as uncial monoalphabets like Libra (1938) and the sans serif Simplex (1939). His main pupil, Dick Doojes, designed Mercator (1957–61), a font inspired by 19th-century sans serifs and presented to the specialist public by a specimen whose graphics were produced by Crouwel himself. From the early twenties until his death, Jan van Krimpen (1892–1958) worked as head designer for the Enschedé en Zonen foundry in Haarlem, devising such austere and severe typefaces as Lutetia (1925), Romanée (1928), Romulus (1931), Van Dijk (1934) and Spectrum (1952). His pupils included figures such as Sem Hartz (van Krimpen's successor at the Enschedé en Zonen in Haarlem and author of, among others, the Juliana face in 1958), Chris Brand and Bram de Does (designer of the triple typeface Trinité in the seventies).

In the second half of the 20th century, we cannot overlook the figure of Gerrit Noordzij, a prominent teacher at the KABK, the Royal Academy of Fine Arts in The Hague, and typographical theorist (see, for example, his *The Stroke of the Pen*, KABK, The Hague 1982), as well as designer of fonts like Remer. His influence was responsible for the formation of a team of designers active in The Hague, including Just van Rossum and Erik van Blokland, authors of the famous Beowolf (1990), Petr van Blokland, Peter Verheul and Gerrit's son Peter Matthias Nordzij. Another exceptional figure in the second half of the 20th century was Gerard Unger, a collaborator first of Crouwel and then of the Enschedé en Zonen and finally a freelance designer of typefaces such as the Demos family (1976), Praxis (1977), Flora (1980) and Swift (1985), as well as lettering for signs for the Amsterdam subway and the Jubilee 2000 in Rome. At the Academy of Fine Arts in Arnhem—Unger's native city—where experts on publishing graphics of the caliber of Jan Vermeulen and Karel Martens have taught, another notable group of Dutch type designers was formed, including Evert Bloemsma, Martin Majoor and Fred Smeeijers.

Alongside this strong current of type design of classical inspiration (in the sense that its practitioners have specific professional skills, developed and matured in the field), the Netherlands has also seen the emergence of avant-garde research into typefaces, fiercely modern and reductive in its approach, which (between the teens and the twenties) had its principal exponents in two members of the Neoplastic movement, neither of whom had any specific training in the field of lettering: Bart van der Leck, who returned throughout his career to a face of his own invention (circa 1917) that was completely disarticulated in its joints; and Theo van Doesburg, the true leader of De Stijl, who developed a rigidly geometric typeface (circa 1919), an uppercase

above: *M Lauweriks*, mark developed out of a spiral by Johannes Matheus Lauweriks (Roermond 1864, Amsterdam 1932), 1912.
right: *Alphabet*, digital reworking of the original by Theo van Doesburg (Christiaan Emil Marie Küpper, Utrecht 1883, Davos 1931), 1919.
right: *De Stijl*, cover of issue no. 2 of the magazine, 1917, by Vilmos Huszar (Budapest 1884, Harderwijk 1960) and Theo van Doesburg.

ABCDEFGHIJKLMNOPQRSTUVWXYZ

monoalphabet of "exact mathematical accents" that had a lasting influence in modern circles, starting with the Bauhaus, where van Doesburg attempted to teach, limiting himself to an external course (1921–22) that left a deep mark on the German school. Another important factor in this radical approach to type was the work of the graphic designer Theo Ballmer in the later twenties.

In reality, it has to be acknowledged that there is nothing new about the Dutch influence on German design. Peter Behrens, an outstanding figure in the arts of the 20th century in Germany (and the designer of important fonts in the first few decades of the century), was made director of the school of arts and crafts in Düsseldorf in 1903.

From 1904 his work was strongly influenced by the compositional re-searches of the architect and theosophist J.L.M. Lauweriks, whom he appointed a teacher at the school in Düsseldorf (after trying in vain to obtain H.P. Berlage). Truly a key figure in the geometrical research founded on the concept of modular grid and elementary iteration, on a methodology of proportions in the "spirit of the time" and of system-atic aesthetics applied to architecture, the applied arts and decora-tion, in the second decade of the century Lauweriks began designing a geometric alphabet from which descend, directly or indirectly, all the subsequent experiments in the radical simplification of letters. His teaching was based, moreover, on design manuals written by his friend and partner Jan Hesselt de Groot, in use for decades from 1896 in Dutch schools and taken up subsequently by other teachers. Significantly this was the sort of text from which Crouwel studied his grammar of forms when he was training in Groningen (he still has it in his personal library).

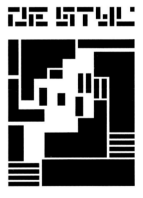

So we have brought to an end this study that has covered the whole span of the 20th century and constitutes the historical context of the "new alphabet." New leads may be suggested, however, by reading Crouwel's article on the tradition of lowercase letters in the Nether-lands ("Lowercase in the Dutch Lowlands," in *Octavo*, 1988, 5, pp. 6–13) or the lecture he gave in The Hague in 1996, centering largely on the history of the "new alphabet" ("Regarder, apprendre, savoir... douter," in *Etapes graphiques*, December 1996, pp. 33–8). And in conclusion, it is worth going back to ponder the interrupted reflec-tions of Roland Barthes on the inner nature of the letter in *Variations sur l'écriture*: "The letter is precisely something that resembles noth-ing: its very nature is to inexorably elude any similarity; the absolute in-tention of the letter is counter-analogical. Of course this is an extreme statement, since everything ends up being like something (and what resembles nothing ends up having an affinity with a letter). So we have to consider that the letter is not 'unconnected' with the pictogram, but that it is opposed to it."

Wendingen, back and front cover of issue no. 10 of the magazine, dedicated to Diego Rivera, 1929; designed by Vilmos Huszar. *Wendingen* was, along with *De Stijl*, the principal Dutch avant-garde magazine, edited by Hendrikus Theodorus Wijdeveld (The Hague 1895, Amsterdam 1987)—an original exponent of the Amsterdam school—who made it the object of typographical experimentation (including "Japanese" packaging), entrusting the extraordinary series of covers to excellent artists from various currents.

matthew carter a man of characters

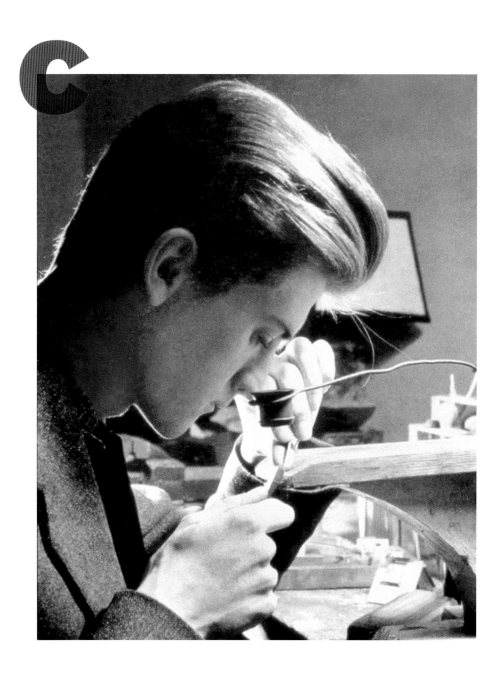

The motto *non flere non indignari sed intelligere*, proclaimed by Baruch Spinoza in the magnificent Dutch 17th-century, its *Gouden Eeuw* (golden age), clearly expresses the rational-abstract hubris that was the enduring legacy of the *esprit de géométrie* transplanted by René Descartes into the fertile philosophical and practical ground of the Netherlands, his second and true home. Spinoza's motto could very well be inscribed on an imaginary academic *resumé* of Matthew Carter.

The great designer, in fact, must be given the credit firstly for an elastic, shaping intelligence, the ability to test and choose the instruments and technologies forged by the unceasing evolution of modern production, without any fear or senseless nostalgia. He adapts them to the constant demands for effective expression and communicational form made on any human artifact that is neither banally cosmetic nor futilely modish, but the product of a rational ethics of the work of design. Remaining in the same philosophical environs, it would be appropriate to assign to Matthew Carter's over forty-year-long career as a designer of characters the borrowed title of *etica more geometrico*.

Born in Britain in 1937, he followed in the family tradition, perhaps predestined to have the father he did (Harry Carter, the well-known historian of the art of punches and lead type as well as archivist at the estimable Oxford University Press). Matthew began his apprenticeship to the profession—as luck would have it— in the Netherlands, not yet twenty years old and just out of school, with vague plans for university (Oxford, of course). The year he spent in the strict school of the venerable Enschedé foundry and publisher, where he learned the art of cutting punches from Jan van Krimpen's assistant P.H. Rädisch, must have been an intense and illuminating experience—how to put it?—on the road to Haarlem, to judge by the results. In fact, after passing the entrance exams for Oxford soon after, he rejected its conservative and rather stale academicism ("English at Oxford was all Beowulf," recalled Matthew Carter, in an interview in 1996, "nothing modern.") He then embarked on an extraordinary career in the arts of printing, supported to his surprise by his type-loving father.

It would take too long to recount his story analytically and accurately, as it deserves and has not yet been done in full. Suffice to say that for six years, following his experience in the Netherlands, Matthew Carter worked as a freelance type and lettering designer in London (his semi-bold Dante, executed under the direction of John Dreyfus and Giovanni Mardersteig, dates from 1961). He then became a consultant to Crosfield Electronics (British distributor of the primordial Photon/Lumitype. This brought him into contact with the Parisian firm Deberny & Peignot and its artistic director, the revered Adrian Frutiger). He was just in time to tackle the transition from lead punches to optical

Matthew Carter (London 1937) at the age of twenty, engraving a punch in steel.

masks and then pixels for the first industrial phototypesetter. In 1965 Carter moved to the New World: he worked for Mergenthaler-Linotype in New York, where he met Mike Parker and Cherie Cone, designing the fonts Snell Roundhand (legitimate offspring of the new possibilities for ligature offered by photocomposition) and Helvetica Compressed, as well as various others, including Greek and Korean typefaces.

Six years later (do his biorhythms run in cycles of six?), Carter returned to London, while keeping his close ties with Linotype. His next typefaces were Galliard (a redesign of the 18th-century characters by Robert Granjon, expressing an eminently Cartesian spirit, as commonly understood, executed in collaboration with Mike Parker, his future partner in Bitstream), Bell Centennial (a classic case study in problem solving, completed in the centennial of the gigantic Bell Telephone Company), Shelley Script and many others, in Hebrew, Greek, Devanagari... From 1980 to 1984 Matthew Carter also held the high position of Typographical Adviser to Her Majesty's Stationery Office and in 1982 was appointed—a great honor—Royal Designer for Industry by the extremely stuffy Royal Society of Arts.

The combination of these events awakened in Carter a hitherto unsuspected entrepreneurial flair. In 1981 he was one of the four founders of Bitstream (*omen nomen*) Inc., one of the first—if not the very first—"independent digital font foundries" in the world, based in Cambridge (Massachusetts). There followed new vectorial founding instruments, new typefaces for use in PostScript, first of all Charter (devised for the low resolution of the early laser printers and thus closely related to Charles Bigelow and Kris Holmes's Lucida and Sumner Stone's Stone Sans).

About ten years later, Matthew Carter and Cherie Cone—two of the founding partners of Bitstream Inc., in difficulties for a variety of reasons, not least that of having a catalogue with over a thousand fonts, most of them in the public domain, licensed to around three hundred companies—set up a new business, Carter & Cone Type Inc., again based in Cambridge. This was the last period (in the chronological sense, *ça va sans dire*) of painfully refined and sensitively interpreted characters in the history of scripts (natural and artificial), experimentally fusible and provocatively radical like Alisal, Big Caslon, Elephant, Mantinia ("I think he [Andrea Mantegna] is the best letterer of any painter"), Miller,

above: texts set in 9/11 pt.
ITC Charter BT roman
10/11 pt. *Bell Centennial address.*

212

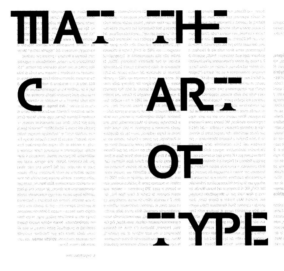

Lecture	→ MATTHEW CARTER	City	→ PESARO -ITALY
Date	→ 24-04-1999	Design	→ LEONARDO SONNOLI
Place	→ DOLCINI ASSOCIATI	Type	→ WALKER + BELL CENTENNIAL

Poster for a lecture
by Matthew Carter designed
by Leonardo Sonnoli in 1999
using the *Walker* and *Bell
Centennial* typefaces.
Printed on both sides
of a sheet of tracing paper.

Matthew Carter, uomo di caratteri

"Più a comprendere appieno l'arte solo chi non le importa una finalità estetica né simbolica, perché essa è assai più che un aspetto di eccitazione estetica e, più che illustrazione, è linguaggio al servizio della conoscenza"
Konrad Fiedler, **Aphorismen**, 36

Il **non fiere non indignari sed intelligere**, proclamato e reclamato da Baruch Spinoza, nel grandioso corso del secentesco Gouden Eeuw (il Siglo de Oro neerlandese), ben esprime la **hybris razional-astratta** che è distunto pertato dell'**esprit de géométrie** impiantato da Renato Cartesio nei fertili terreni filosofico-pratici dei paesi bassi, sua seconda è vera patria; a buon dritto, il motto spinoziano potrebbe trovar posto in esergo a un immaginario medaglione accademico di Matthew Carter. A merito del grande designer va, infatti, ascritta in primis una elasto-plastica intelligenza progettuale, ossia la capacità di adottare (mettendoli a selettiva prova) strumenti e tecnologie forgiati dal rincorrersi incessante dell'evoluzione produttiva moderna, senza tema alcuna né inutili nostalgie, tanto quanto di adattarli alle assidue necessità di espressione prestazionale e di conformazione comunicazionale, proprie di ogni artefatto umano che non sia né banalmente cosmetico né fultimente modiolo, bensì meta ed esito di una razionale etica del lavoro progettuale. Restando nei medesimi dipressi filosofici, all'ultra-quarantennale carriera di disegnatore di caratteri di MC si potrebbe dunque appropriatamente attribuire anche il titolo impresato di **ethica more geometrico**.

Classe 1937, nato nel Regno Unito di Sua Graziosa Maestà Britannica, in certo senso figlio d'arte, perciò forse predestinato dalla sorte stessa d'avere un padre quale il suo (Harry Carter, noto storico dell'arte dei plumbei secolari tipi da stampa, nonché archivista presso la degnissima Oxford University Press), il nostro Matthew inizia il suo apprendistato professionale – ve-

dicaso – in Olanda, non ancor ventenne e fresco di scuola superiore, con vaghi piani universitari (Oxford, of course). L'internato d'un anno presso la scuola severa della venerada officina type-editoriale Enschedé, ove impara l'arte d'incider punzoni con PH Rädsch, assistente di Jan van Krimpen, dev'esser stata per MC esperienza di intensa folgorazione, come dire? sulla via di Haarlem, a giudicare dagli esiti successivi. Infatti, superati di lì a breve gli esami d'ammissione all'esclusivissimo ateneo oxfordiense, il nostro ne rifiuta l'accademismo conservatore e un po' stantio ("English at Oxford was all Beowulf," – ricorda MC, al proposito, in un'intervista del 1996 – "nothing moderno") per intraprendere una straordinaria carriera nelle arti della stampa, supportata con sua sorpresa dal tipofilo padre. Troppo lungo sarebbe qui rintracciare analiticamente e puntualmente la vicenda, come merita e ancor non c'è forse fatto appieno. Basti sapere che per sei anni, dopo l'esperienza olandese, MC lavora come Freelance Type & Lettering Designer a Londra – del 1961 il diventare nel 1963 consulente della Crosfield Electronics (distributore inglese della primeva Photon/Lumitype: MC entra così in contatto con la parigina Deberny et Peignot e il direttore artistico della medesima, il venerabile Adrian Frutiger), affrontando per tempo il passaggio dai punzoni per il piombo alle maschere ottiche e ai successivi pixellaggi per la prima fotocompositrice industriale. Nel 1965, MC si trasferisce nel Nuovo Mondo: lavora a New York per la Mergenthaler-Linotype, ove incontra Mike Parker e Cherie Cone, disegnando i caratteri Snell Roundhand (figlio legittimo delle possibilità nuove di legature della fotocompositrice) e Helvetica Compressed, oltre a vari altri tipi, ad esempio greci e coreani. Sei anni dopo (che i suoi biciolini siano esannupli?), MC torna a Londra, mantenendo stretti legami con la Linotype; è la volta dei tipi Galliard (un redesign delle secentesche forme di Robert Granjon,

espressivo d'uno spirito eminentemente carteriano, nella ricezione comune, eseguito in collaborazione con Mike Parker, futuro sodale anche nella Bitstream), Bell Centennial (un classico caso-studio di "problem solving", completato nel'anno del centenario della gigantesca Bell Telephone Company), Shelley Script e di molti altri, ebrei, greci, devanagari... Dal 1980 al 1984, Carter è chiamato anche alla alta responsabilità di Typographical Adviser to Her Majesty's Stationery Office, la stamperia di stato britannica (com'è brutalmente distante la situazione del nostro paese da tutto ciò, ancora...) ed è nominato nel 1982 – grande onore – Royal Designer for Industry dalla compassatissima Royal Society of Arts. Nel concerto di questi eventi, si rinveglia in Carter una inedita **vis** imprenditoriale; nel 1981 è tra i quattro fondatori della Bitstream (omen nomen) Inc., una delle primissime – se non proprio la prima delle – fonderie digitali indipendenti al mondo, con sede a Cambridge (quella in Massachusetts, Usa, non quella omonima e originaria, in Uk): nuovi strumenti di forgia vettoriali, nuovi tipi da disegnare in PostScript, per primo il Charter (ideato per la bassa risoluzione delle prime stampanti laser ed perciò garante stretto del Lucida del duo Charles Bigelow & Kris Holmes e dello Stone Sans di Sumner Stone). Una decina d'anni dopo, Matthew Carter e Cherie Cone – due dei partner fondatori della Bitstream Inc., in difficoltà per ragioni varie, non ultima di avere in catalogo di oltre 1000 caratteri, in massima parte di pubblico dominio, dati in licenza a circa 300 produttori – avviano una nuova impresa, la Carter & Cone Type Inc., di-dem. È il periodo ultimo (in senso cronologico, ça va sans dre), di caratteri crudelmente raffinati e sensibilmente interpreti della storia delle scritture (naturale e artificiali), sperimentalmente fusivi e provocatoriamente radicali, quali Alisal, Big Caslon, Elephant, Mantinia ("I think he (Andrea Mantegna) is the best letterer of any painter!"), Miller, Sophia (bizantinamente ibrido e impronte di cupo), Walker (un inedito bastoncino graniabile

da tastiera, per il trainante Walker Art Center di Minneapolis, Usa). La Carter & Cone Type Inc. ha anche pragmaticamente sviluppato su commissione tipi per Apple, "Sports Illustrated", "Time", "Us News & World Report", "Wired"; da incarico, i caratteri per il www dell'internet, cioè dei veri tipi da schermo (compatibili con normali requisiti di hardcopy), commessi dal "gigante cattivo" Microsoft: Georgia e Verdana – provare per credere! Conclusione provvisoria, meditabonda e augurale. Non prima di una finale citazione del nostro: "(disegnare) un carattere è sempre una sorta di lotta tra la natura alfabetica della forma delle lettere, la A/tà delle A, e il desiderio di mettere qualcosa di tuo; è un conflitto tra la rappresentazione di qualcosa (non puoi prenderti libertà smodate nel disegno delle lettere) e la tensione di ritrovarvici un ette di te stesso". **Ars longa, vita brevis**, parrebbe avvisarci l'attività perdurante del nostro carattere Matthew Carter, oggi acuto Senior Critic (due per tutte, delle sue osservazioni recenti, riportate dal bravo J Abbott Miller: "movable type is now mutable type" e "technology changes faster than design") presso la Yale's Graphic Design Faculty, a monito di chi voglia intraprendere (con studio, applicazione e passione) l'arte sublime e sottilissima dei punzoni attuali, ancor prendere per poco si vorrebbe, nel Bel Paese che vide attivo tempo addietro un certo Francesco Griffo (manigoldo sambra, quanto geniale punzonista del soave umanista-imprenditore Aldo Manuzio, tanto per rammemorare due almeno, de' nostri, chè la lista sarebbe lunga assai) ed è oggi nuovamente ostello di sparuta, incerta ma (assicuro e testimonio di persona) agguerrita – più di quanto non s'immagini massa stessa – truppa di letteristi novissimi. Lunga vita a quest'arte antica, erga, in cui fumo eccellentissimi: fervidi intensi auspici (spero condivisi) di progettuali patrii ricorsi, in una visione della storia che per l'umillimo scrivente non conosce ripetizioni, **strictu sensu**, ma consente dei ritorni, forse.

© Sergio Polano 1999

City	← PESARO>ITALY
Design	← LEONARDO SONNOLI
Type	← WALKER + BELL CENTENNIAL
Lecturer	← MATTHEW CARTER
Date	← 24-04-1999
Place	← DOLCINI ASSOCIATI

Poster for a lecture by Matthew Carter designed by Leonardo Sonnoli in 1999 using the Walker and Bell Centennial typefaces. Printed on both sides of a sheet of tracing paper.

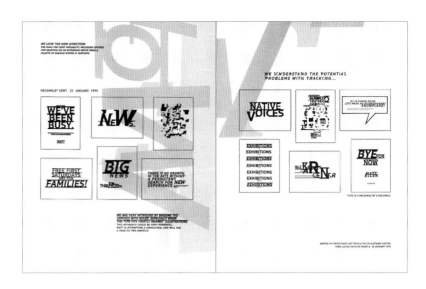

Walker, specimen
of the typeface, 1998; designed
for the Walker Art Center
of Minneapolis.

MANTINIA

AABBCCDDEE
FFGGHHIIJJ
KKLLMMNN
OOPPQQRRSS
TTUUVVWW
XXYY&&ZZ
1234567890

MANTINIA™

This titling face is meant for use at display sizes. The letters are based on inscriptional forms, inspired by those painted and engraved by the Italian Renaissance artist Andrea Mantegna (c.1431–1506). Mantegna's fascination with classical antiquity, splendidly shown in an exhibition last year, led him to be one of the first to revive Roman lettering.

MP HE LP TT MD E CME

Mantinia has some "inscriptional" characters not normally found in type: 16 ligatures, four tall capitals, 13 small capitals, and a complete alphabet of superior capitals kerned to combine with the regular caps. (Please note that we recommend setting Mantinia only in a program that supports kerning.) The font includes an interpoint and two leaves.

LI AR QU LM RT To &C

Mantinia was designed by Matthew Carter. It is combined here with ITC Galliard Roman as a text face. MANTINIA is a trademark of Carter & Cone Type Inc. Fonts for the Mac & PC are available from Carter & Cone at 2155 Massachusetts Avenue, Cambridge MA 02140, and by telephone at 800 952-2129 &617 576-0398, fax 617 354-4146.

JANUARY•1993

MANTINIA
DESIGNED
CARTER•AND
TO•ANDREA
ARTIST•AND
MANTEGNA
ENGRAVED
EPIGRAPHIC
OF•ANCENT
REVIVED•BY

A•TYPEFACE
BY•MATTHEW
DEDICATED
MANTEGNA
ANTIQUARY.
PAINTED•&
THE•ROMAN
LETTERING
MONUMENTS
HUMANISTS

Mantinia, specimen of the typeface, 1993; some solutions for the glyphs were suggested by the letters carved on the front of the Boston Public Library, 1892 (architect C.F. McKim). The term glyph (from *glyphé*, carving) signifies anything engraved in a hard material, and is customarily used for pictograms and hieroglyphs. For many centuries, designing typefaces meant making them material, i.e. carving them in metal: the art of the punchcutter. It was also very common for punches of many variants, or different glyphs, to be made for a single letter or other character. Carter has gone back to probing the question of glyphs (and ligatures) in digital form as well.

ULLMAN THINKS IT WAS POGGIO WHO BEGAN THE PASSIONATE STUDY OF CLASSICAL INSCRIPTIONS TO WHICH SEVERAL GIFTED ITALIANS DEVOTED THEMSELVES LATER IN THE CENTURY. SOME OF THEM WERE NOT SCRIBES: CIRIACO OF ANCONA, ANTIQUARY, ANDREA MANTEGNA, PAINTER, LEON BATTISTA ALBERTI, ARCHITECT, AND ONE WHO WAS AN ANTIQUARY AND SOMETHING OF A SCRIBE, FELICE FELICIANO. THEY WERE CONCERNED WITH REVIVING THESE LETTERS IN ARCHITECTURE RATHER THAN IN BOOKS. FELICE'S ENLARGED DRAWINGS OF TYPICAL ROMAN CAPITALS BASED ON CLASSICAL EXAMPLES LED TO A SERIES OF ATTEMPTS TO CONSTRUCT THE LETTERS BY RIGID GEOMETRY BEGINNING WITH A BOOKLET BY DAMIANO MOYLLE OF ABOUT 1480 AND GOING ON LATE IN THE SIXTEENTH CENTURY. WHEREAS THE CAPITALS OF BLACK LETTER COULD BE & WERE WRITTEN VARIOUSLY AND DIFFERED FROM PLACE TO PLACE AND WERE NOT IN THE CHILDREN'S ALPHABET-BOOKS, THE HUMANISTIC SCRIPT WAS TIED TO THE ROMAN CAPITALS AND WAS INFLUENCED BY THEM INCREASINGLY.

THE EXTRACT OPPOSITE IS TAKEN FROM 'A VIEW OF EARLY TYPOGRAPHY' BY HARRY CARTER OXFORD·1969 PAGE 46

Sophia (Byzantinely hybrid and densely somber) and the brilliant Walker (one of the very few truly in keeping with our times, an unprecedented font with "snap-on" serifs for the keyboard, designed for the Walker Art Center in Minneapolis, US. Carter & Cone Type Inc. has also programmatically developed fonts to commission for Apple, *Sports Illustrated*, *Time*, *US News & World Report* and *Wired*. Noteworthy are their fonts for the World Wide Web, i.e. authentic "typefaces for the screen" (compatible with some of the requirements of hardcopy), commissioned by the giant Microsoft: Georgia and Verdana—try them and see! Provisional, meditative and auspicious conclusion. But not before a final quotation from Matthew Carter: "[Designing] a typeface is always a sort of struggle between the alphabetic nature of the form of the letters, the A-ness of As, and the desire to put in something of your own. It is a conflict between the representation of something (you can't take inordinate liberties in the design of letters) and the tendency to find a bit of yourself in it." *Ars longa, vita brevis* seems to be the message of the enduring activity of the man of characters Matthew Carter, now acute Senior Critic at Yale's Graphic Design Faculty. (Two of his recent comments, cited by the able J. Abbott Miller, will serve for all:

ITC Galliard BT roman
ITC Galliard BT italic
ITC Galliard BT bold
ITC Galliard BT bold italic
ITC Galliard BT ultra
ITC Galliard BT ultra italic
ITC Galliard BT black
ITC Galliard BT black italic

"movable type is now mutable type" and "technology changes faster than design").

His work admonishes all who, armed with study, application and passion, wish to take up the sublime and very subtle art of today's punches, namely the design of digital typefaces. A thankless art, but let us hope things will change soon here in Italy, which saw a certain Francesco Griffo at work many centuries ago (he was a scoundrel it seems, as well as a brilliant punchcutter for the gentle Aldus Manutius, just to recall two of our own). Now it is once more home to a small, insecure but experienced troop of new letter designers. Long life, therefore, to this ancient art, in which we were once eminent, and our most fervent wishes for its return to the homeland of design, in a vision of history—that of the humble writer—which may not admit of repetitions in the strict sense, but perhaps permits returns.

Verdana regular
Verdana italic
Verdana bold
Verdana bold italic

above: texts set in
9/11 pt. *ITC Galliard BT roman*
7.5/11 pt. Verdana.

erik spiekermann the identity of berlin

"In order to be effective every organization needs a clear sense of purpose that people within it understand. They also need a strong sense of belonging," declares Wally Olins in the introduction to his classic work on the subject, *Corporate Identity*. Here he is responding to the question: what does identity mean for institutions? "Purpose and belonging are the two facets of identity. Every organization is unique, and the identity must spring from the organization's own roots, its personality, its strengths and its weaknesses. This is as true of the modern global corporation as it has been of any other institution in history, from the Christian church to the nation state." To a great extent, suggests Olins elsewhere, these "identities" are directed and guided by the instruments of communication. For many contemporary businesses, the design of their image and the communication of their identity are considered the most appropriate and powerful of the resources available for their growth, as demonstrated by the investments they are willing to put into them. However, the "image coordination" of human institutions and organizations is not a recent phenomenon nor one exclusively confined to the world of business, industry and the market. Sticking for simplicity to the 20th century, we should not overlook, in the sphere of business, the exemplary and in some ways pioneering work of AEG in Germany, whose "image" (meaning products, buildings and communication in general) was defined and coordinated from 1907 onward by Peter Behrens, a many-sided exponent of modern visual thinking and among much else a remarkable designer of typefaces.

On the other hand, in the communication of the image of public corporations and the design of information of "public utility" (to use an ambiguous definition now in vogue), the examples of the London transport system and the Dutch post office are equally emblematic of the design of identity. The consortium of the London Underground, later London Transport, under the guidance of Frank Pick (1878–1941), who became its commercial manager in 1912, played a role of the greatest significance in the history of contemporary design. In 1915 Pick was one of the founders of the Design and Industries Foundation (a sort of British Werkbund). Among his many merits was the adoption of Underground Railways Sans, the typeface he commissioned in 1916 from Edward Johnston, one of the greatest calligraphers of all time, used from 1919 on for all the printed signs of the London transport system. Redesigned in digital format and given the name New Johnston it is still in use today. With good reason it can be considered the progenitor of every modern sans serif (Paul Renner's celebrated Futura, for instance, dates from 1927, the same year as Eric Gill's Gill Sans, which took its inspiration directly from Johnston's alphabet). Then there was the adoption in 1933 of Henry Beck's "map," the prototype of every modern diagrammatic representation of transport networks, not just subways (though it was not immediately appreciated); the involvement of artists ranging from Frank Brangwyn to Edward McKnight Kauffer

Erik Spiekermann (Stadthagen 1947), 1995.

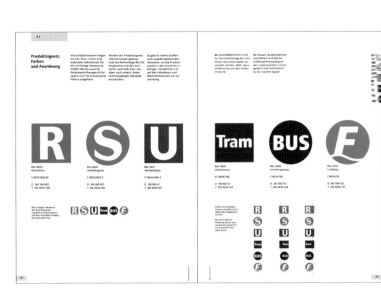

Produktsignets: Farben und Anordnung

Die Proportionen von Hoheitszeichen, Logo und Firmierung

Das Logo und andere Zusätze

BVG Berliner Verkehrsbetriebe

BVG Gut für Sie. Und Berlin.

BVG Service

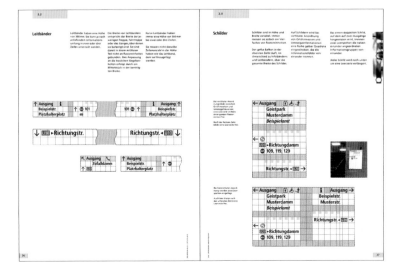

Leithänder

Schilder

Informations-
und Leitsystem

BVG

Berliner
Verkehrsbetriebe

Basiselemente

BVG

Berliner
Verkehrsbetriebe

U-Bahnhof

BVG

Berliner
Verkehrsbetriebe

left: pages from coordinated-
image manuals for the Berliner
Verkehrsbetriebe, the Berlin
public transport system,
1987 on; examples
of application: symbols
distinguishing the type
of transport, the logotype, signs.
above and left: covers from
coordinated-image manuals for
the Berliner Verkehrsbetriebe.

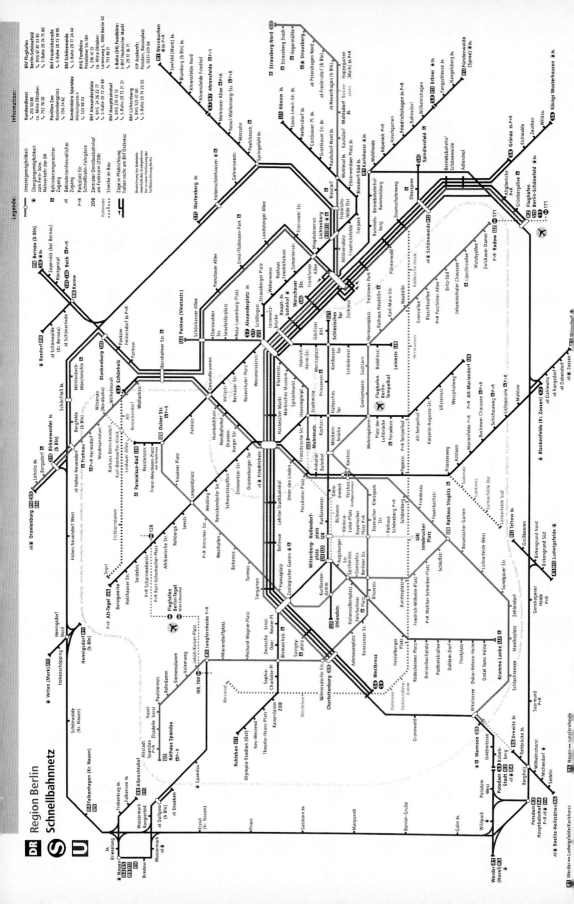

and even Man Ray in the design of refined company posters; the commissioning of Charles Holden to design innovative subway stations, like Arnos Grove or Cockfosters, and the head offices of the Underground, with controversial work by Jacob Epstein and Henry Moore.

Equally important, for communication of "public utility," was the new direction imparted to the Dutch Post Office by Jean-François van Royen (1878–1942). After denouncing the poor quality of public communication in 1912 ("thrice horrible: horrible lettering, horrible composition, horrible paper; horrible the three main elements that define the aesthetic quality of printed matter"), he succeeded over three decades in designing a coordinated image of the highest level for the institution. He did so by calling on the best design talents in the country (including K.P.C. de Bazel, M. de Klerk, V. Huszar, G. Kiljan, W. Penaat, J. Crouwel, P. Zwart, P. Schiutema, L. van der Vlugt and W.H. Gispen), establishing an enduring tradition of information design in the Low Countries whose exceptional vitality and quality is almost unparalleled in Europe, and which has nothing to do with graphics and advertising as we normally understand them.

The recent, sophisticated operation of the design of the "identity" of Berlin, carried out by Erik Spiekermann, is in its turn part of a consolidated tradition of experience in the communication of a public image in postwar Germany (with the notable cases, for example, of Kiel, Leipzig, Leverkusen and Ulm). Berlin is, however, the outstanding case, especially with the opportunity provided by the reunification of the country and the capital. In the sixties, in fact, it was one of the main exponents of visual design in Germany, Anton Stankowski, who devised a well-known system of identity for the city, adopted for a quarter of a century and known as the Berlin-Layout. In essence this was a grid with the logo "Berlin" composed in Helvetica at fixed points, which defined "principles of conception tending to render the visual identity of Berlin uniform, at least on the plane of graphics. All the printed matter of the administration should be, over time, perfectly identifiable, without ambiguities. It should be possible to say: this is a letter, a program, a brochure, a poster for Berlin!"

In 1992 the Berlin senate held a competition by invitation for the Berlin-Identität, the city's new image, in which Ivan Chermayeff (New York), Pentagram (London), Mendell&Oberer (Munich), MetaDesign (Berlin), Eberhard Stauss (Munich) and Jean Widmer (Paris) took part. The impeccable and monolithic project entered by Widmer, a pupil of Itten and the author—among much else—of the coordinated image of the Centre Georges Pompidou (1974) and the Musée d'Orsay (1983, with Bruno Monguzzi), was awarded first prize. His "image" was characterized essentially by the choice of a pictogram as symbol of the city, the leaf of a lime tree (an obvious reference to Unter den Linden), and the use of Frutiger as the institutional typeface. Spiekermann with MetaDesign earned an honorable third place; but in 1994 he was given the commission, after some controversy.

The map of the Berlin transport system designed by MetaDesign; it is an evolution of the classic "circuit" scheme conceived by Henry Beck for the London Underground in 1933.

The system of signs
in two subway stations.
As well as making a decisive
contribution to the image
of the new Berlin, Erik
Spiekermann has also designed
Meta, the most successful
typeface of the nineties:
a highly distinctive
"modulated sans serif."
right, text set in 9/10.5 pt.
Meta plus book.

This was probably due to the persuasive and flexible attitude he displayed during the competition. On that occasion, MetaDesign declared that for the communication of the Berlin-Identität it rejected the "Prussian military method, widely practiced all over the world, which consists in drawing up a manual, a collection of suggestions and prohibitions." Instead it appealed "to common sense, reason and perhaps also a sense of economy." Spiekermann's image of the city, which was an attempt to convey the dynamism of Berlin's culture and the changes under way there, was defined through a sophisticated system of complementary elements: the spiral as a generating symbol and irregular "windows" that break through the print surface, the motto Berlin and the bear as an emblem, a range of colors in which a traditional red predominates, formats based on a ratio of 2:3 and a module of 12 × 18 mm, and finally a family of typefaces developed for the purpose, called Berlina. Since 1994, the so far partial implementation of Spiekermann's project for the Berlin-Identität has involved a series of substantial adaptations to circumstances and the requests of the client. This has led to the drafting of a "Basisdesign" for the administration, a repertory in which the "non-schematic system" of the competition project is set out very simply, enabling it to be used by others. This has entailed the design of a new symbol for the city (the image of the Brandenburg Gate associated with the logo Berlin, composed in the Thesis typeface), a closely related range of colors, the mixed use of two fonts (Myriad, a contemporary digital sans serif, and Berthold Garamond, an evocation of tradition). So far, the beneficiary of the new image has been the BTM, Berlin Tourismus Marketing GMBH, a public agency set up specifically to develop tourism in the city. After trying out a series of start-up samples of printed matter commissioned directly from MetaDesign, it is now proceeding independently. At the same time, the system of communication designed by MetaDesign for BVG, the Berlin public transport system, a project begun in 1987, is now taking shape. The complex visual machinery extends from the standardized logo to a vast range of pictograms, digital typefaces (Bvg, Concorde, Frutiger), signs, information points, network maps in diagrammatic form and the decoration and furnishing of stations. With exceptional results for the time in which we live, Spiekermann has carried out an accurate, consistent and delicate task of information design for the BVG, an exemplary and up-to-date demonstration of the importance of visual quality in communication of "public utility." Perhaps it will stimulate reflection and comparison with the situation in Italy, currently disastrous but not without opportunities for improvement in this respect.

Meta plus book SMALL CAPS
Meta plus book oblique SMALL CAPS
Meta plus medium SMALL CAPS
Meta plus medium oblique SMALL CAPS
Meta plus bold SMALL CAPS
Meta plus bold oblique SMALL CAPS
Meta plus black
Meta plus black oblique

left: *In Synthesis Berlin*, cove of guide no. 7, July 1995.
below: construction
of the symbol for the city
of Berlin, which associates
the logotype (set in the *Thes*
typeface) with a stylized ima
of the Brandenburg Gate.
right: the flexibility
of the possible chromatic
and compositional
combinations of the symbol
for the city of Berlin is teste
in this collection.

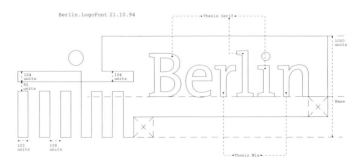

tibor kalman and the heat goes on…

They're hard to forget, the graphics on the cover of the Talking Heads' LP *Remain in Light* and the lyric sheet (from which I've taken the phrase in the subtitle) that came with the record. It was 1980 and the author of the artwork was destined for fame: his name was Tibor Kalman. He left us this spring and his passing was all the more dramatic since he was one of the few members of my generation who had something to say in his own field. Kalman was neither a "graphic artist" nor a designer by training, which in fact changed nothing. In fact it is highly instructive for a country like Italy, where most designers of artifacts are self-taught. Kalman was, rather, an outsider and *sui generis*: "I have no manual skill," he was prepared to admit, a few years ago. "I still can't draw and I don't know how to use a computer."

His avowed goal was "communication," that vast and confused metaphor which has set its stamp on our present civilization. Evidently, avowedly, he was interested in the "contents" and not the "container" (if and when it is possible to disentangle them), in the message rather than the medium—and blow the idea that the medium is the message! For design was just a stage, a process, a tool to be used to get what he wanted: to change the world, at least a little, at least in part: "My Holy Grail is not design, because design is a language, not a message."

He was born in 1949 in Budapest, Hungary, a country that has a great and yet little-known tradition in the field of visual design: think of Huszar, Moholy-Nagy, Farago and Biro, Lajos Kozma and Karoly Kos and, last but not least, Ferenc—Italianized into Franco—Pinter. Kalman met with the classical fate of the *émigré*, when his family moved to the US after the tragedy of 1956.

From 1963 to 1967 he attended Our Lady of Lourdes High School in Poughkeepsie, a place best known as the cradle and headquarters of IBM. In 1967–70 he studied journalism and history at New York University—and met Maira, the woman with whom he was to share his life. His first job was with a bookstore in New York, more or less by chance, as he often said of every event in his existence: it was Barnes & Noble, a chain destined for great commercial success.

From 1968 to 1979, Kalman was responsible for all of Barnes & Noble's corporate communications (window dressing, signs, décor, advertising...). In 1979 he founded M&Co., a true workshop of design, of insatiable and flexible aptitudes, which from the mid-eighties on displayed a remarkable capacity for applied creativity. "M&Co. has no style," explained Kalman, talking about their work, "just a method, founded on ideas." The ideas were sometimes surreal, sometimes sarcastic and often wry, as well as spiced up with pungent provocations. With this spirit and many excellent collaborators, M&Co. was active right through the eighties and into the nineties, operating for fifteen years in ever broader fields, fearlessly exploring and crossing apparent boundaries, using different media and languages, breaking away from the conventional and seeking a witty reappropriation of the vernacular, fertile in its incoherence.

Tibor Kalman (Budapest 1949, Puerto Rico 1999), 1997 in an image manipulated by Massimo Gardone.

right: *November*, cover of menu for the Florent Restaurant, 1986; artificially decontextualized communication lies at the base of many of Tibor Kalman's inventions: the menu of a trendy restaurant— advertised, moreover, without giving its address—is composed with bulletin-board characters like a weather report, with plays on words.
below: in 1983, Tibor Kalman persuaded a firm specializing in accessories for yuppies to produce a series of watches; Tibor Kalman defined the objects designed by M&Co for this market as "yuppie pornography."

So from the traditional domain of printed matter M&Co. moved on to music videos, movie titles, TV spots and the design of objects. Among the things that emerged from his peculiar factory of ideas were watches with the numerals all mixed up or the glass over their dials frosted so that the time was blurred, or that were quintessential like the "ten.one.four"; Magrittean wrappings that declare this is not a hat; postcards representing sectioned stomachs for a restaurant; videos like *(Nothing but) Flowers* for the Talking Heads again, where everything turns on the relationship between the visible word and the group's image. And then there was the firm's collaboration on the project for the reclamation of 42nd Street and Times Square in New York (from the watch to the city, realizing the dream of so much modern design), as well as major works in publishing, such as the art direction of magazines that included *Artforum* (1987–88) and *Interview* (1989–91). Kalman had already grasped one of the central changes underway in today's communication. He saw that "the future of graphics does not lie on the printed page but on the screen."

In 1990 it was the design of a magazine that brought him to Italy: this was *Colors*, an extraordinary experiment made possible by the munificence of Benetton, which made him famous all over the world. Kalman edited the first five issues, from 1991 to 1993, from New York. From 1993 to 1995 he moved with his family (which comprised, along with the faithful Maira, a fine illustrator, his children Lulu Bodoni and Alexander Tibor Dibi M.L. Onomatopeia) to Rome, where he produced eight more issues. The series of *Colors* edited by Kalman terminated with the performance of *Wordless*, an issue made up solely of images, chosen from 25,000 pictures. In autumn 1995, Kalman returned to New York, already ailing.

He went back to work as consultant on an extensive series of projects: the rehabilitation of Lower Manhattan again; exhibition designs for the Whitney Museum (the show "New York: City of Ambition"); inventive publications for Vitra International, from the magazine *Workspirit* to the much praised monograph *Chairman Rolf Felbaum*, already a classic of its kind. He left us, too soon. We would like to recall his spirit by quoting one last, crude comment: "Much of what is communicated is shit. I think that designers should really apply themselves to messages, should start to look at the messages, start to comment on them, start to influence them."

NOVEMBER

SOUP   BOUDIN & WARM TARTS

GUSTY WINDS

HIGH S UPPER 40S TO MID 50S

LOWS UPPER 30S TO MID 40S

FLORENT

OPEN 24 HOURS   989 5779

WATCH FOR HEAVY RAINS

WEAR YOUR GALOSHES

MNCO

above: *Colors no. 4*, retouched
portraits (John Paul II, Arnold
Schwarzenegger, Elizabeth II,
Spike Lee) assembled under
the title *What would happen
if...?*, 1993; the issue
is devoted to racial differences.
right: the masthead
of the magazine.

COLORS

ed fella the vernacular in american graphics

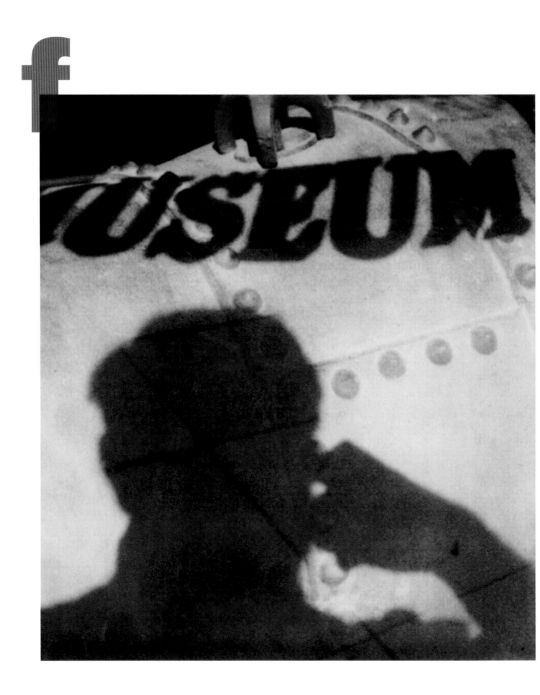

In the disciplines that, following their own divergent paths, scrutinize, investigate, dissect and reassemble the ever-changing and growing body of human history, right down to the centrifugal brink of the present, a significant critical focus on material culture has emerged and been refined in the field over the course of the last few decades. In this approach, history is examined by looking at the widespread culture of the masses rather than that of the elites, at recurrent phenomena rather than exceptional events, at common artifacts rather than art or luxury objects, at the tools and techniques of work and production rather than symbolic and representational constructs, at mentalities rather than great men.

Naturally this approach has produced a reassessment of the crucial question of dialects and vernaculars (which, according to the prevailing definition, are essentially the lexis of dialect), in the strictly linguistic area as well as in the broader field of histories (including those of all the arts). They are no longer regarded as minor, local, erudite studies, so getting beyond the impasse of the mere "environmental" protection and conservation of cultures.

Now that the intrinsically poly-systemic nature of developed languages has been made clear, in every field of expression—each of which turns out to be an accumulation of many languages, interacting on different and not always congruent levels—an attempt has been made to investigate the relations of normative languages (the recorded, shared, standardized repertories of current usage and understanding) to the spontaneous words of dialects and the tenacious roots of oral traditions, in keeping with the objectives and methods of the various disciplines. In fact this type of study has been undertaken by researchers of all sorts, involving the most disparate subjects and spheres, in the Old World as well as the New.

The phenomenon has been particularly marked, in its extent and the results achieved, in the United States, ever since early Pop Art, with the important subsequent developments both in the arts (with graffiti artists, for example) and architecture (a whole new trend in taste, supported by polemically refined theses and virtuoso design performances). In effect, in the US this stance—often mistaken for a sublimated nostalgia and obsession with the trivial—has deeper roots in the dream of an autogenous variety of languages, in claims of autochthony (for a colonial, immigrant culture, of crude, popular European origins, and certainly not for that of the natives, who were dispersed, marginalized and excluded, where they were not exterminated).

It is part, in short, of the cult (at times naive, at times radical in its ancestry) of an American Civilization that in the 20th century produced its most original and interesting results not in high culture but in low: comics, cartoons, movies, commercial art, computer graphics. In particular, American graphic design has always displayed a fascination with the vernacular (we may note, in passing, that the term comes from the Etruscan *verna*: a slave born in the home, hence a servant). The term is especially used for homely craft skills, including an intense recent fascination with anti-design and anti-intellectualism, closely linked to the spurious, the residual, even to "trash."

The continuity of American vernacular in graphics is easy to discern through the decades. We see it in a whole current of illustrators, from Frederic Remington to Norman Rockwell, right down to Milton Glaser and the latest exponents of New Pop, to mention just the first names that come to mind and ignoring the comic strip artists (but how can we forget Walt Kelly's Pogo or Robert Crumb's Mr. Natural?). It also appears in designers of type (whose indigenous peculiarity, a sort of original sin, lies in the frontier exuberance of the Wood Types), from the Bentons to Frederic W. Goudy, William A. Dwiggins, Oswald "Oz" Cooper and Herb Lubalin. It is also exemplified by many of the typefaces in the catalogues of digital foundries, such as Emigré or T26. We could go on like this, listing other designers in tune with the conventionally folksy tone of the vernacular.

To get away from the rigidity of modern stereotypes and shake off the dogma of what appeared, at this point, to be a tired and belated internationalism, contemporary American graphics found it necessary to resort to the authenticity of the naive, "deregulating" the classic visual thinking of European origin, adding inelegant errors of grammar picked up "on the road" and an extreme, random deconstruction of the message, as illustrated by the worldwide success of David Carson. So much of recent US work has been produced under the all-too-conscious banner of this revival of the moods and tones of the street and the neighborhood, of store signs and gas pumps, of torn posters and battered billboards.

All this seems to be going on without these designers having fully grasped the critical reflections on graphic language and the chronicle of the American way of life that lies behind the renewed interest, at a distance of decades, being shown in the vernacular by two key figures in the history of this American tradition of graphics: Saul Steinberg and Ed Fella.

Born near Bucharest, Saul Steinberg, after studying sociology and psychology in the Rumanian capital, took a degree in architecture at the Milan Polytechnic in the thirties and began to work in that extraordinary melting pot of ideas that was Antonio Boggeri's agency. Moving to the US in 1941 (as yet another émigré fleeing persecution), Steinberg invented an incisive, distinctive and highly original

Trash, drawing by Saul Steinberg, n.d.
Who Are They?, drawing by Saul Steinberg, n.d.; both drawings belong to the collection of illustrations **The Discovery of America**, published by Mondadori in 1989 (Knopf, 1992).

238

style of graphics, imitated by generations of illustrators and cartoonists all over the world.

The surreal, intellectual and often acerbic irony of his visual narrative, always sustained by a perfect mastery of expression in spite of an apparent lack of technique and a constant, sophisticated pursuit of primitivism, perhaps reaches its peak in the depiction of the American urban and rural landscape to which he devoted some of his most famous albums (such as *The New World* in 1965 and *The Discovery of America* in 1992). It is no accident that Peter Blake described him as "the finest architecture critic in the world."

Today Ed Fella is another subtle explorer of the panorama of American vernacular and in particular the "landscape of letters," with an eye strongly drawn to the signs of the alphabet, the typologies, colors and reflections of common scripts.

Professor of visual design at the famous CalArts in Valencia, California, Fella is a belated experimental educator. Declaring provocatively "I hate fine anythings" and suggesting that his students adopt an attitude of "disturbance, distraction and distortion" in order to avoid any fetishistic and solipsistic sophistication of communicative artifacts, Fella has become the principal source of inspiration for the latest generation of graphic artists and type designers in the US.

At the center of his complex approach to aesthetics, under an informal-casual guise, is a programmatic "More into Less," aimed at superseding both the "Less is More" of modernist sobriety and the "More is More" of postmodernist excess. His work and his teaching are characterized by a series of deliberate manipulations, carried out with the precise aim of amplifying and modifying the "message." This has set a widely followed example and made a real impact on the whole of today's graphics.

On the composition of texts, for instance: the irregularity of the spacing between letters and words; the cutting off of parts of the letters; scalar alignments; repetitions, false new lines and undulations; irregular variations of body and "color" in typefaces.

Accepting the hypothesis of "design as discourse" (shared by the most perceptive American visual designers), Fella is telling us that we have to unlearn what we know to regain, through tempered license, a playful, joyful and humorous approach to narration in contemporary graphics.

Typographic compositions
drawn with biro in four colors,
n.d.

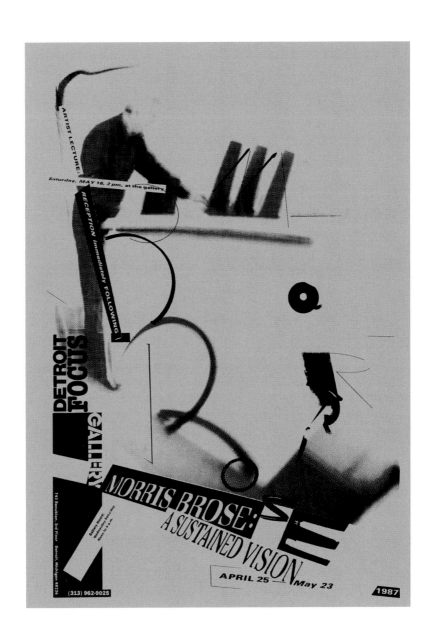

left: *Polaroids*, n.d.
above: *Detroit Focus Gallery*,
bill, 1987.

left: *Polaroids*, n.d.
above: *Detroit Focus Gallery*,
bill, 1987.

abstr action

juror: al   loving
january 6 - feb ruary 3   1989

detroit focus gallery
OPENING RECEPTION:JANUARY 6 5-8:30PM
743 beaubien 3rd floor
detroit michigan 48226
(313) 962-9025

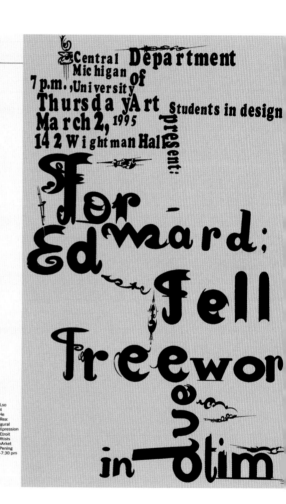

Central Department
Michigan of
7 p.m.,University
Thursda yArt Students in design
March 2, 1995
14 2 Wi ght man Hall present:

for-ward;
Ed fell
freewor
in ptim

aLso
iN
tHe
aRea:
figural
eXpression
dEtroit
aRtists
mArket
oPening
5-7:30 pm

244

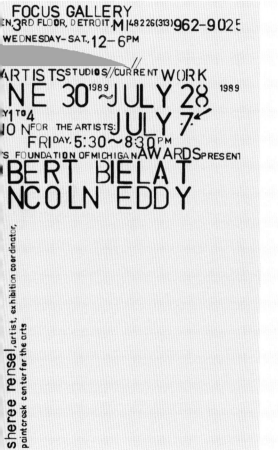
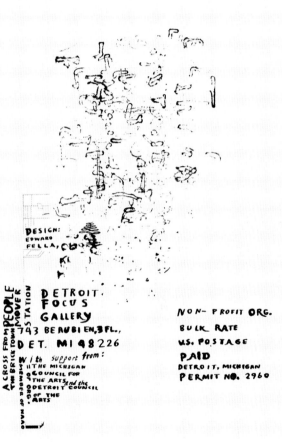

from left: *Detroit Focus Gallery*,
bill, 1989.
For/Ed/ward Fella: Freework
in due time, bill, 1995.
Detroit Focus Gallery, bills,
1989.

Publishing Credits

Typology
The Characters of the Visible Word
Apart from a few trivial corrections, this is the text published in Italian under the title "Tipologia" in *Casabella* (Milan), 668, June 1999, pp. 68–75, and, with more substantial revisions, the one published in English with the title "Typology" on pp. 88–89.

Paper Architecture
The Graphics of Stamps
Apart from some slight modifications and minimal abridgments of the Italian text, this appeared under the title "Architetture da incollare" in *Casabella* (Milan), 660, October 1998, pp. 36–41. English text first appeared in the same issue with the title "Paste-on Architecture." I returned to the theme in the article "Minimo design pubblico," in *Sintesi* (Perugia), 11, December 2000, no page nos.

Talking Figures
The Art of Illustration
In a slightly longer version than this one, it can be found (in English and Italian) in the catalogue of the exhibition "New Pop," Palazzo Fortuny, Venice 1994, edited by Giorgio Camuffo, Edizioni Arti Grafiche Friulane, Venice-Udine 1994, under the title *Talking Figures. Parlanti figure*, no page nos. The text has been retranslated from the Italian for this book.

The Return of Pictograms
Semiosis Dresses Up
With a few specific references to authors of pictograms, omitted in this version, it was published in Italian under the title "La semiosi si camuffa" in *Sintesi* (Perugia), 10, October 2000, no page nos.

Posters
Notes towards an Imaginary Entry in a History of Visual Thought or, more precisely, of the Printed Artifacts known as Posters
Originally written for the poster of a presentation, it has been published in a longer version in Italian, under the title "Cartelloni. Disegno industriale del manifesto," as an introduction to the graphic work of Leonardo Sonnoli, in *Dezine* (Treviso), 1, May 2001, pp. 10–11.

Digital Soup
Culture of the CD-ROM?
Partial text of the speech at the symposium *L'editoria digitale*, promoted by the Municipality of Venice, held in Mestre, April 10, 1996.

Peter Behrens
Zeitgeist and Letters
In essentially identical form, with the title "Zeitgeist: le lettere di Behrens," it appeared in Italian in *Casabella* (Milan), 678, May 2000, p. 86.

El Lissitzky
The Electro-Library of the Constructor
Published, with minimal differences, as "L'elettrobiblioteca del costruttore" in Italian in *Casabella* (Milan), 680, July–August 2000, p. 88.

Alexander Rodchenko
Advertising-Constructor
More or less the same text has been published in Italian, with the title "Costruttori pubblicitari," in *Casabella* (Milan), 682, October 2000, p. 92.

Eric Gill
Stone Carver
Without significant variations, it can be found in Italian as "Eric Gill / Stone Carver" in *Casabella* (Milan), 686, February 2001, p. 84.

Jan Tschichold
Faith and Reality
This is the text published in Italian, under the title "Fede e realtà," in *Casabella* (Milan), 688, April 2001, p. 94.

Kurt Schwitters
Merz ist Form: the Art of Typography
The text has been published in Italian in *Sintesi* (Perugia), 16, February 2002, no page nos.

Bauhaus
Type, Typography, Typophoto
Written especially for this volume.

Paul Renner & Paul Rand
Two 20th-Century Masters
An Italian version with minimal variations has been published, as "2 × PR," in *Casabella* (Milan), 676, March 2000, pp. 85–6.

Wolfgang Weingart
From Nieuwe Beelding to New Wave
In essence, this is the text published (as part of a feature on Wolfgang Weingart) in Italian with the title "Dal Nieuwe Beelding al New Wave" and in English with the title "Wolfgang Weingart. From Nieuwe Beelding to New Wave" in *Casabella* (Milan), 655, April 1998, pp. 48–63, which I enlarged on in the speech *Ascesa e crisi of the "grafica svizzera,"* introduction to Wolfgang Weingart's' lesson, given in the ISIA conference hall in Urbino, on May 6, 2000. I returned to the subject of Weingart in "L'arte tipografica di Wolfgang Weingart," in *Sintesi* (Perugia), 9, June 2000, no page nos.

Max Huber
Notes on Concrete Abstraction
This text is (with a few cuts) the original version of the article that appeared (in English) as "Max Huber. Thinking Through Images," in *Affiche* (Arnhem), 9, April 1994, pp. 46–51, published *partim*, with the title "Max Huber. Pensare per immagini," in *Casabella* (Milan), 650, November 1997, pp. 78–85 (Italian and English). The text has been retranslated from the Italian for this book.

Adrian Frutiger
Petite Histoire de l'Univers
Without many differences, published as "Petite Histoire de l'Univers" in *Casabella* (Milan), 669, July–August 1999, p. 84.

Aldo Novarese
The Italian Way of Type
I have devoted a series of texts to the great Italian typographer, commencing with the essay, written with Pierpaolo Vetta and published in English, "Aldo Novarese: Letters Are Things" in *émigré* (Sacramento), 26, spring 1993, pp. 30–37, and continuing shortly afterward with "Aldo Novarese. Progettare l'alfabeto" in *Arte Documento* (Udine), 7, 1993, pp. 339–44 (apart from a few revisions and abridgments, this text is the version published here). Two of my texts came out *in memoriam*: the short "So long, Aldo!" (in English), in *TypeLab Gaczeta* (Barcelona), September 1995, 3, p. 2, and (using parts of the previous texts) "Aldo Novarese letterista 1920–1995," in *Casabella* (Milan), issue 0, December 1995, pp. 44–47—the latter, *idem* in *Casabella* (Milan), 632, March 1996, pp. 46–49 (an obituary that I had written in 1996 for *Abitare* has remained unpublished). More recently, an article of mine on Novarese, entitled "Alfa-beti: sintesi di scrittura e figura," came out in *Sintesi* (Perugia), 8, March 2000, no page nos.

Giovanni Pintori
Effect of Synthesis
The text has been published, in a slightly longer version—under the title "Pintori, *Omen Nomen*"—by *Sintesi* (Perugia), 12, February 2001, no page nos.

Franco Grignani
Gestaltung
On Grignani and his phototypographic research I have published a text (in English) entitled "The Gestaltung Primacy," in *HQ High Quality* (Heidelberg), 3, 1995, pp. 34–39 (in the German edition of the same magazine, "Das Primat der Gestaltung"). This version is not related to the article in *HQ* but is an abridgment of the obituary "Franco Grignani (1908–1999)" written for *Casabella* (Milan), 667, May 1999, p. 80.

Wim Crouwel
Lowercase in the Lowlands
This is the text prepared, between 1999 and 2000, for a reprint of the *new alphabet* in an Italian version, a work still in progress.

Matthew Carter
A Man of Characters
This text was originally printed on the recto of the poster designed by Leonardo Sonnoli, on the occasion of a meeting with Carter at Pesaro on April 24, 1999. Brought out, almost unchanged, as "Matthew Carter, uomo di caratteri" by *Notizie Aiap* (Milan), 10, June 2000, pp. 41–42, it has been published, with a few modifications, again as "Matthew Carter, uomo di caratteri," in *Casabella* (Milan), 690, June 2001, pp. 76–83 and 95 (and in English, with the title "Matthew Carter. Man of Characters"). The text has been retranslated from the Italian for this book.

Erik Spiekermann
The Identity of Berlin
Published, in an almost identical version, under the title "L'immagine della città," in *Casabella* (Milan), 634, May 1996, pp. 2–11 (Italian and English). The text has been retranslated from the Italian for this book.

Tibor Kalman
And the Heat Goes On…
Obituary published in Italian, in a slightly longer version, as "And the heat goes on…," in *Casabella* (Milan), 670, September 1999, p. 84.

Ed Fella
The Vernacular in American Graphics
After presenting the work of Ed Fella, in the ambit of *Wanted Creativity*—a Fabrica initiative—held at Catena di Villorba (Treviso) on June 14, 1997, I published in Italian (in a version with minimal variations) the essay "Ed Fella, lettere dall'America" in *Casabella* (Milan), 658, July–August 1998, pp. 50–61 (and in English, with the title "Ed Fella, Letters from America," substantially revised for this book).